The Best Of
Faiz Ahmed Faiz

The Best Of
Faiz Ahmed Faiz

Selection and English Translation by
Kuldip Salil

ISBN : 9788170287919

Ist Edition : 2009, 6th Reprint : 2020

BEST OF FAIZ (Urdu Poetry) by Faiz Ahmed 'Faiz'

Selected and translated by Kuldip Salil

RAJPAL & SONS

1590, Madarsa Road, Kashmere Gate, Delhi-110006
Phone : 011-23869812, 23865483, 23867791
e-mail : sales@rajpalpublishing.com
www.rajpalpublishing.com
www.facebook.com/rajpalandsons

To
My father, Shiv Lal, Advocate
who was classfellow with Faiz
at Murray College, Sialkot

Introduction

Punjab has produced a number of great poets, not only in Punjabi and its various dialects, but in Urdu as well. Of the Urdu poets, two names stand out and vie with the best in the language. Most obviously, they are Mohammed Iqbal and Faiz Ahmed Faiz. Faiz was twenty seven years old when Iqbal died and it can be said without hesitation that the mantle of greatness, passed on from one to the other. Faiz, who was a great admirer of Iqbal, is indeed the greatest Urdu poet after Mir, Ghalib and Iqbal. Sajjad Zahir, a noted writer and critic, writing on just one of the poetic collections of Faiz, 'Dast-e-Saba', says that it was the most important event of 1953 in Pakistan.

Born in Sialkot in West Punjab on 11th February, 1911, Faiz was a mild mannered, soft-spoken man who would rather let others talk than talk himself. His father, Sultan Mohammed Khan was a lawyer who had earlier served Amir Abdul Rehman in Afghanistan and had acquired courtly habits. Later, he incurred the displeasure of his master, and had to flee Afghanistan. His next port of call was England from where he took his degree in law and came back to his native country. Like his father, Faiz too was an adventurer, but he was a traveller more of the mind than space. He read books and journals and travellers' tales and attained a firm grounding in the ideas and cross-currents of the nineteenth century. He was rooted in his soil rather than travelling to Europe, as was the fashion among the scions of well-to-do families those days, and as his famed predecessor Mohammed Iqbal had done. He breathed the air of his country and knew its people more intimately than most others.

Sultan Mohammed died in 1931 and his landed property became a subject of litigation among Faiz's brothers. The poet scruplously kept away from all this. He, in fact, left the village alongwith his mother. Much later, in 1955 when his brother died, he went back to the village and distributed the land among the tillers, retaining only half an acre for himself and his dependants.

An ineptitude for the affairs of the world is a well-known trait of most creative artists. Ghalib put it succiently when he said :

फ़िक्रे-दुनिया में सर खपाता हूँ
मैं कहाँ और ये वबाल कहाँ

Worrying about the world, I wrack my brain
O for a man like me, an endeavour how vain

Faiz gave proof of this quite early in life. Indolence seems to be another quality shared by many poets. John Keats is the best example of it. Faiz says that one thing he found very difficult was replying to letters. Unlike many other poets, however, Faiz was averse to self-projection. "I hate to speak about myself," he says, "So much so that I avoid the use of first person singular I always use 'we' for this." He was a shy person, who unlike Iqbal and Firaq, recited his poems quite badly. It was, of course, more than made by the quality of his verse.

Faiz's early education like that of most children from Muslim families started with recitations from the Quran and the study of Urdu, Persian and Arabic. The word 'Faiz' means bounty. Apart from studies and love of poetry, Faiz Ahmed Faiz was interested in dawdling and playing cricket, among other things. He was first admitted to the madarsa of Maulvi Ibrahim and later moved to Scot Mission School after which he joined Murray College, Sialkot For higher studies, he went to Govt. College Lahore, from where he took BA (H) degree in Arabic in 1931. He obtained a Master's degree in English literature in 1933. He post-gratuated in Arabic also.

Before coming to Lahore, Faiz was already feasting on the poetry of Mir, Ghalib and Daagh. At Murray College in Sialkot, Faiz tried his hand at writing poetry in English, apart from Urdu poetry. He was a voracious reader of the novels of Dickens and Hardy.

In Lahore, Faiz got greatly immersed in the cultural and intellectual atmosphere of the Govt. College, where among his teachers and friends were Pitras Bukhari of All India Radio fame and eminent poets and critics like Mohammed-ul-din Taseer and Sufi Ghulam Mohammed Tabassum. Also, he came in close touch with Hafeez Jallandhri, Akhtar Sheerani, Chirag Hasan Salik and Imtiaz Ali Taaj—all well known in their field. It was under the influence of Hafeez Jallandhri, Akhtar Sheerani and Hasrat Mohani that Faiz started writing poetry. Those were leisurely times and educated young men could indulge in long hours of debate in the coffee house and on the bank of river Ravi in the moonlight.

After finishing his studies, Faiz joined Oriental College Amritsar in 1935 as lecturer in English. He later took up lecturership in the same subject at Hailey College of Commerce, Lahore.

In 1941, Faiz married Alys George, an English socialist. Alys was a woman of remarkable character, who was a friend and companion to Faiz. She and their two daughters gave stability to his otherwise tumultuous life. Faiz was once invited to speak on Shakespeare in a womens' college where a screen stood between the speaker and the audience. He felt both amused and indignant. In such an atmosphere marriage with Alys was indeed a blessing.

In 1941, Faiz resigned his teaching job and joined the British Indian Army, more out of his hostility towards Fascism than any loyalty to the British. In 1947, he resigned from the army and took up the editorship of 'Pakistan Times' and 'Imroze', both progressive papers.

Four years later in 1951 an event took place which not only changed the course of Faiz's life but also put his life in great danger. Faiz, alongwith Sajjad Zaheer, a leading light of Progressive Writers' movement in India, and two other army officers was arrested on charges of complicity to overthrow the legally established government of Pakistan. He was sentenced to more than four years of rigorous imprisonment, out of which, he was in solitary confinement for three months. These three months he spent in Sargodha and Layalpur jails, where he was completely cut off from the outside world; not even his wife and children were allowed to meet him.

During the trial, though his life always hung in a balance. On the final day of that trial he was actually told by his lawyer that he would most probably get death sentence. Faiz, not only remained calm, he did not show any anxiety at all. He smoked and laughed and joked with his fellow prisoners as before, say some of the other inmates in the jail. According to one inmate while outside, it was cries of 'death for the traitors,' inside the jail, Faiz and colleagues were on a virtual picnic.

फ़िक्रे-सूदो-ज़िया तो छूटेगी
मिन्नते ईनो-आं तो छूटेगी
ख़ैर दोज़ख में मय मिले-न-मिले
शेख साहब से जाँ तो छूटेगी

I will be free from worrying about gain and loss at least
And will not have to please all and sundry,
I may or may not get wine in hell
I shall be at least rid of the Sheikhji

These years of incarceration, however turned out be kind of a blessing in disguise for Faiz. They were, creatively the most fruitful years of his life. A large number of poems of 'Dast-e-Saba' and 'Zindan Nama' were written in this period and remain the crown of his poetic achievement. It was in the course of the trial in the conspiracy case, known as the Rawalpindi case, that he read out this famous couplet :

वो बात जिसका सारे फ़साने में ज़िक्र न था
वो बात उन पे बड़ी नागवार गुज़री है

That which was never a part of the story
That bit has piqued him immensely

and made the judge speechless.

Life in the jail, however, can at times be nerve-wrecking and can even lead to mental breakdown. As a safety valve, some of Faiz's fellow prisoners tended to quarrel and created ruckus. In these circumstances, poetry writing came as a great relief for Faiz. But life in the jail certainly took its toll. This is evident from many a couplet, though he tried to put up a brave front and used the experience to good account :

जो तुझसे वादा-ए-वफ़ा उस्तवार रखते हैं
इलाजे-गर्दिशें लैलो-निहार रखते हैं

Those who have pledged firm loyalty to you
Make light of the sufferings that this path entails

Faiz was ultimately released from jail in April 1955 and soon after that he resumed the editorship of 'Pakistan Times' and 'Imroz'. In 1956, he attended the Afro-Asian writers' conference in Tashkent. In the meantime, there was an army coup in Pakistan when General Ayub Khan ousted Iskandar Mirza in 1958. Consequent upon this coup, Faiz's progressive papers were taken over by the martial law regime and Faiz was once again arrested in 1959. Making false cases against individuals, was not uncommon those days. Even in the Rawalpindi conspiracy case, the government prosecutor himself later told Faiz and his collegues in the jail that while it was true that they had met, talked and decided not to stage the coup, they had failed to destroy their papers, which were seized by the government and a mountain was made of a molehill. The reason, according to Major General Akbar Khan, was that the government was not happy with some of military officers and wanted to get rid of them and their friends.

Faiz who had been arrested by the martial law regime under the Safety Law was released in 1959. In the same year, he was appointed the Secretary of Lahore Arts Council, a position he held till 1962. In this year, he won Lenin Peace Prize and in the next, travelled extensively to Egypt, Lebanon, Algeria, Hungary, England and Russia. In 1965, he joined the Department of Information as honorary adviser. Later he was associated with the Institute of Literature and Culture. During the premiership of Benazir Bhutto, Faiz won Pakistan's highest award Nishan-e-Pakistan. This award was given posthumously. He was an active member of Afro-Asian Writers' Council and worked for their journal 'Lotus.'

In 1977, Pakistan saw another army coup, the third, in which General Zia-Ul-Haq overthrew the regime of Zulfikar Ali Bhutto. Faiz's poetry was banned on Pakistan radio and TV. He went into a voluntary exile and was away from Pakistan from 1978 to 1982 alongwith his wife. During this period, he spent some time in Beirut when the Palestenian struggle was at its peak, and wrote some of his most moving poems :

Lullaby for Palestinian Children

Do not cry, my child
Your mother has just slept after weeping a long while,
Do not cry, my child
Only some time back, your father has departed
Relieved of all sorrow,
Do not cry my child,
Your brother is away to an alien land
And your sister has gone away the same way,
Do not cry my child,
They have just bathed the dead sun and buried the moon in your courtyard,
Do not cry my child,
For, if you cry,
Your mother, father, brother and sister
Alongwith the sun and the moon
Will make you cry all the more.

And if you smile
There is a real possibility.
That all of them in disguise
Will come and play with you.

Faiz had a mission to fulfill - the raising of peoples' awareness, not only in the sub-continent but the world over. In this sense, he was citizen of the world and the entire world was his stage. In any case, great men and creative geniuses belong to all mankind.

In 1982, Faiz returned to Pakistan. He was suffering from asthma which was aggravated by his unsettled life and disturbed existence. In 1984, he fell ill and was admitted to Mayo Hospital, Lahore where he passed away on 30th November, 1984. Both progressives and conservatives were keen to own him up and show that Faiz was their poet. There were slogans both of 'Inqlab Zindabad' and 'Nara-e-Tadbeer'. In this context one is reminded of Kabir, after whose death both Hindus and Muslims vied with each other to claim that he belonged to them.

Faiz's poetry portrays people's lives, their hopes and aspirations, their heartbreaks, hardships and frustrations with a rare elegance and beauty. And his lyricism lends a unique charm to that poetry. Also, Faiz's poetry reflects the noblest human sentiments and values in the midst of gloom engendered by the exploitation and oppression of the masses and their miserable life. And these values are perfectly in consonance with the time-tested values of the sub-continent.

According to a senior critic, Asar Lakhnavi, Faiz is the greatest progressive poet; his imagination and art raised his verse to great heights. He has presented delicate feelings in an exquisite form. His popularity in both India and Pakistan and the world over is a testimony not only to his greatness but also his ability to establish a rapport with the people. In fact, he is a people's poet.

The depth and delicacy of Faiz's poetry, owes a lot to his deep study of classial literature. According to Firaq Gorakhpuri, Faiz blends his love-experience with struggle-related social issues, endowing Urdu poetry with a new splendour and introducing in his love poetry a completely new and acceptable element. Coming from Firaq, who is himself a master of love poetry, this is a great compliment.

Faiz's poetry received strength and sustenance from the plight of the common people and their struggle to improve their lot. He championed their cause most eloquently. The poignancy and power of his poetry derives largely from a blend of his boundless love for groaning humanity and his personal sufferings! It is a poetry not only genuine and spontaneous, it has an authenticity about it which wins a ready response from the audience.

Another reason for the tremendous appeal of his poetry is a glimpse of hope for the bright dawn, born out of the womb of the night of gloom, the night symbolising oppression, helplessness and sufferings. It is not a Utopia that Faiz is presenting; it is a light after having gone through the tunnel, a triumphal glimpse after a struggle, at least on the mental plane. And courage perseverance and call to the collective might of the people are the weapons of this struggle :

चले चलो कि वो मंज़िल अभी नहीं आई

Press on, for the destination has not yet arrived

He suffered, but he hoped that the struggle and sufferings will not go in vain:

जो हम पे गुज़री सो गुज़री मगर शबे-हिज्रां
हमारे अश्क़ तेरी आकबत संवार चले

Whatever befell us, O evening of separation, was part of the game But our tears brightened you up all the same

Faiz perfected the art of presenting contemporary themes in the classical garb. He uses conventional images, symbols and metaphors of Urdu poetry to express contemporary concerns. And he invests these images and symbols with new meanings. A great admirer of Ghalib and classical scholars and poets, he knew, as we all know, how great a sway the ghazal has had on all lovers of poetry from eighteenth century onwards. So, he wrote not only fascinating ghazals observing all its rules, even his nazms have a sweetness and charm of the ghazal. Of course, whenever necessary, he uses free verse also, but even his free verse reads like good poetry rather than perverted prose. In fact, he was instinctively against prose poetry. He said he did not understand it; it should rather be called poetic prose.

Faiz was a leading light of the Progressive Writers' Association, a movement launched at a convention in Lucknow in 1936 presided over by Munshi Premchand. It was a movement that spans about half a century and dominated the literary scene in the sub-continent. Apart from political reasons, socialism was a new mantra that the idealists could use against the enemies of communalism—which was spreading fast in Punjab and elsewhere - by uniting the people against the common enemy—poverty. Almost a decade before partition, communal riots had started erupting in the sub-continent. PWA was catching the imagination of the writers, and Faiz was an active member of its Punjab branch. He spent his evenings teaching workers the three R's and elementary politics. It was a good means of remaining in touch with the people and knowing their life at first hand.

He has been called 'enlightened human socialist' by some people. His socialism is not dogmatic; it adapts to the needs of the times. His papers 'Pakistan Times' and 'Imroze' became a mouthpiece of progressive views and protest against anti-people policies of the state. He was the president of Pakistan Peace Committee and Trade Union until his arrest in 1951.

Faiz was a committed writer, a champion of the neglected and downtrodden with a burning desire to change the social order. He was a socialist by conviction and paid a heavy price for this conviction. He was, attacked not only by his opponents who charged him with treason and sent him to jail, but even by his own people, his comrades and fellow socialists. As great a poet as Ali Sardar Jafri, who is himself a great champion of the socialist cause, launched a scathing attack on Faiz, saying that the kind of poetry that Faiz was writing could be written by any "Jan Sanghi or Muslim League" poet. Says Faiz :

चश्मे-नम, जाने-शोरीदा काफ़ी नहीं
तोहमते-इश्क़ पोशीदा काफ़ी नहीं
आज बाज़ार में पाबजौला चलो
शहरे-जाना में अब बावफ़ा कौन है
दस्ते-क़ातिल के शायां रहा कौन है

रुख्सते-दिल बांध लो, दिलफ़िगारो चलो
फिर हमीं कत्ल हो आयें, यारो चलो

Moist eyes are not enough, not the tortured soul,
Nor would the allegation of concealed love do
Go to the marketplace in fetters today

Who else is pure enough in the city of the beloved
Except us
To win the assassin's hand ?
Take your sorrowing heart with you, let's go
Once again
O comrades, let's go and be slain

And this hostility came inspite of Faiz's unshakable belief that poetry must serve a cause; it should serve as a "beacon to poor humanity's afflicted will" and must not merely display flights of fancy and ornamental skills. The attack by Sardar Jafri and some other progressive writers was indeed an unkind cut, although one cannot accuse Jafri of jealousy.

Although, as the cliche goes, comparisons are odius, it is tempting to compare Faiz with at least one of his contempories and one great predecessor. The contemporary was Firaq Gorakhpuri. Firaq is a great modern poet of the ghazal and one of the greatest in the genre. He has sometime been called the emperor of the ghazal which remains his forte, in spite of the fact that he wrote some good nazms and a large number of rubais, some of which are most memorable. Faiz, on the other hand, though he is equally good in his ghazals, has a place of pre eminence in Urdu poetry because of nazms. If Firaq has a demon in the heart, which must come out through his poetry, Faiz is fired by a mission. Firaq is essentially a poet of the individual, a poet of the restless mind, whereas Faiz is looking outside in the society around. Both are progressive poets, but in their own way.

One more difference between the two is that, while in Faiz, one cannot pick out many poems and say that they are below a certain level and should not have formed part of his published work, it is not so in the case of Firaq. Many of his early poems are indeed sub standard; they look like the work of a learner and should not have been included in his collections.

Another point of difference between Firaq and Faiz is that the former is largely a poet of love and beauty, and in this he scales great heights. He has the power to stir your imagination and make it soar :

हंसते खेलते मैखाने में आये थे फिराक़
जब पी चुके शराब तो संजीदा हो गये

We came to the tavern in a playful mood, O Firaq
But became serious after we had drunk wine

Faiz, as against this, presents a wonderful blend of love poetry and poetry of social concern. Both Faiz and Firaq have given Urdu poetry some memorable poems, though in Firaq's case his output is uneven. Perhaps Firaq wrote his best poems in his later life, as hinted earlier, whereas Faiz has written great nazms and ghazals both in his later and early period particularly when he was in jail. His later poetry acquires a new power because of transnational concerns, especially when Pakistan lost its eastern part, and East Bengal had great resentment against Pakistan.

The predecessor to be compared with Faiz is Mohammed Iqbal. Both Faiz and Iqbal were dissatisfied with the prevailing state of affairs; they were critics of society and sought to change it. Both were fired by an overriding and compelling faith. A remarkable thing about Faiz and Iqbal is that both succeed in transforming the raw day-to-day events into great poetry. For Iqbal, however the new millennium lay in his vision of a revival and renewal of Muslims and a pan Islamic movement, whereas for Faiz, the panecea lies in socialism. Iqbal recalled the memories of Muslims, the world conquerors, Faiz seeks a synthesis between woes of the hard-pressed toiling classes and the grief of the lovers. Both sought a world vision to sustain their work but these visions are different. If a philosophical framework for Faiz is to be found in Karl Marx, Iqbal too had admired Marx in more than one poem, but his emphasis was elsewhere.

One of the major differences between Faiz and Iqbal is that whereas Iqbal is direct, ardent and impetuous, Faiz is soft and suggestive. Unlike Iqbal, he is not a god, speaking down to his awe-struck audience; he is one of them, a man speaking to man who quietly makes his way into their hearts. If Iqbal is like Milton, Faiz is like Wordsworth in this respect.

Faiz not only acknowledged Iqbal's greatness and wrote on him, he also helped to make a documentary on his life and work. In this context, one is reminded of a memorable observation of John Dryden. Writing of Shakespeare and Milton, he says that we admire Milton, but we love Shakespeare. One may as well say, we admire Iqbal, we love Faiz. Iqbal's great couplet,

हज़ारों साल नरगिस अपनी बेनूरी पे रोती है,
बड़ी मुश्किल से होता है चमन में दीदावर पैदा

For ages the Narcissus bewails its purblind state
The birth of a discerning eye is an event rare and great

applies as much to Iqbal himself as it applies to Faiz.

October 1, 2009 **Kuldip Salil**

Contents

The Best of Faiz

मता-ए-लौहो-कलम[1] *छिन गयी तो क्या ग़म है*
कि खूने-दिल में डुबो ली हैं उंगलियां मैंने

ज़ुबां पे मोहर लगी है तो क्या, कि रख दी है
हर एक हल्का-ए-ज़ंजीर में[2] *ज़ुबां मैंने*

Mata-e-Loho-kalam chhin gayee to kya gham hai
ki khoone-dil mein dubo li hein ungaliyan maine

Zuban pe mohar lagi hai to kya, ki rakh di hai
har ek halk-e-zanjeer mein zuban maine

---

1. कलम और तख्ती रूपी दौलत 2. ज़ंजीर के हर एक हिस्से में

I care not
if I stand divested of the pen and the tablet,

I have dipped my fingers
in the blood of my heart,

What if my lips are sealed, for I have
Put a tongue through my chain in every part

गुलों में रंग भरे बादे-नौबहार[1] चले
चले भी आओ कि गुलशन का कारोबार चले

क़फ़स[2] उदास है यारो, सबा[3] से कुछ तो कहो
कहीं तो बह्रे-खुदा[4] आज ज़िक्रे-यार चले

बड़ा है दर्द का रिश्ता, ये दिल ग़रीब सही
तुम्हारे नाम पे आएंगे ग़मगुसार[5] चले

जो हम पे गुज़री सो गुज़री मगर शबे-हिज्रां[6]
हमारे अश्क़ तेरी आक़बत[7] संवार चले

मुक़ाम[8] 'फ़ैज़' कोई राह में जंचा ही नहीं
जो कूए-यार से[9] निकले तो सूए-दार[10] चले

(जेल में लिखी ग़ज़ल)

Gulon mein rang bhare bade-naubahar chale
chale bhi aao ki gulshan ka karobar chale

Qafas udas hai yaro saba se kuchh to kaho
kahin to behare-khuda aaj zikre-yaar chale

Bara hai dard ka rishta, ye dil gharib sahi
tumhare naam pe aayenge ghamgusar chale

Jo hum pe guzari so guzari magar shab-e-hizra
humare ashq teri aaqbat sanwar chale

Maqaam 'Faiz' koi raah mein jancha hi nahin
jo kuche-yaar se nikle to sue-daar chale

---

1. नव-वसन्त की हवा 2. पिंजरा 3. प्रभात-समीर 4. भगवान के लिए 5. हमदर्द 6. वियोग की रात को 7. परलोक 8. स्थान 9. यार की गली से 10. फांसी के तख़्ते की ओर

So that the flowers flush with colour,
so that the spring breeze starts blowing
Do come now, so that the garden's business gets
going

The cage lies desolate, O friends, appeal to the
breeze:
Let there be some talk of the beloved somewhere,
please

The bond of suffering is strong indeed, the poor
heart notwithstanding
For your sake they'll come again, though my
comforters are now going

Whatever befell us, O evening of separation, was a
part of the game
But our tears brightened you up all the same

No other place, O Faiz, appealed to me on the way
As I left my beloved's lane, my road straight to the
gallows lay

दुआ

आइये हाथ उठायें हम भी
हम जिन्हें रस्मे दुआ[1] याद नहीं
हम जिन्हें सोज़े-मुहब्बत[2] के सिवा
कोई बुत कोई खुदा याद नहीं

आइये अर्ज़-गुज़ारें[3] कि निगारे-हस्ती
ज़हरे-इमरोज़[4] में शीरींनी-ए-फ़र्दा[5] भर दे
वो जिन्हें ताबे-गिरांबारी-ए-अय्याम[6] नहीं
उनकी पलकों पे शबो-रोज़[7] को हल्का कर दे

जिनकी आँखों के नहे-सुबह का यारा[8] भी नहीं
उनकी रातों में कोई शम्मा मुनव्वर[9] कर दे
जिनके कदमों को किसी राह का सहारा भी नहीं
उनकी नज़रों में कोई राह उजागर कर दे →

Aaiye hath-uthayen hum bhi
hum jinhen rasmen dua yaad nahin
hum jinhen soze-muhabbat ke siva
koi but koi khuda yaad nahin

Aaiye arz-guzaren ki nigare-hasti
zehre-imroz mein shireeni-e-pharda bhar de
woh jinhen tabe-giranbari-e-ayyaam nahin
unhin palkon pe shabo-roz ko halka kar de

Jinki aankhon ke nahe-subah ka yara bhi nahin
unki raaton mein koi shamma nunavvar kar de
jinke kadmon ko kisi raah ka sahara bhi nahin
unki nazron mein koi raah ujagar kar de

---

1. प्रार्थना 2. प्रेम में जलन 3. प्रार्थना करें 4. आज का ज़हर 5. कल की मिठास 6. जीवन का बोझ सहने की ताकत 7. रात-दिन 8. आशा 9. रोशन

A Prayer

We who worship no idol, no God,
Rememeber not the manner of prayer,
Know nothing except the warmth of love,
Let us raise our hands and pray

That those whose today is bitter
May have sweet tomorrow;
Courtesy life's beauty,
Pray, make the lives of those oppressed
by the burden of life
Light and happy;

Those who have no hope for the dawn
Illuminate their nights,
Show them the way who know not where to go

→

जिनका दीं पैरवी-ए-ग़ज़बो-रिया[1] है उनको
हिम्मते-कुफ्र मिले, जुर्रते-तहकीक मिले
जिनके सर मुन्तज़िरे-तेग़े जफ़ा[2] हैं उनको
दस्ते-कातिल को झटक देने की तौफ़ीक़[3] मिले

इश्क़ का सिर्रा-ए-निहां[4] जाने-तपां है जिससे
आज इकरार करें और तपिश मिट जाये
हर्फ़े-हक[5] दिल में खटकता है जो कांटे की तरह
आज इज़हार करें और ख़लिश मिट जाये

Jinka din pairavi-e-gazhbo-diya hai unko
himate-kufra mile, zurrate-tehqik mile
jinke sar muntzire-tege zafan hai unko
daste-qatil ko jhatak dene ki taufiq mile

Ishq ka sirra-e-nihan jaane-tapan hai jisse
aaj iqrar karen aur tapish mit jaye
hurphey-huq dil mein khatakta hai jo kante ki tarah
aaj izhaar karen aur khalish mit jaye

1. झूठ और फ़रेब 2 ज़ुल्म की तलवार 3. ताकत 4. छिपा हुआ भाग 5. सच्चाई

And expose the lies and hypocrisy, in the name of
religion, perpetrated.
Those, over whose heads hangs the sword of the
tyrant
Give them the courage to shake away the assassin's
arm,

May the secret of love which is scalding the soul
Be out and there is relief,
May the word of truth, which pricks the heart like
a thorn
Be proclaimed, and anguish disappears

रक़ीब से

आ कि वाबस्ता[1] हैं उस हुस्न की यादें तुझ से
जिसने इस दिल को परीख़ाना[2] बना रक्खा था
जिसकी उल्फ़त में भुला रक्खी थी दुनिया हमने
दह्र को[3] दह्र का अफ़साना बना रक्खा था
आशना[4] हैं तेरे क़दमों से वो राहें जिन पर
उसकी मदहोश जवानी ने इनायत की है
कारवां गुज़रे हैं जिन से उसी रा'नाई[5] के
जिसकी इन आंखों ने बेसूद[6] इबादत की है
तुझसे खेली हैं वो महबूब[7] हवाएं जिनमें
उसके मलबूस की[8] अफ़सुर्दा[9] महक बाक़ी है
तुझ पे भी बरसा है उस बाम से[10] महताब का[11] नूर[12]
जिस में बीती हुई रातों की कसक बाक़ी है
तूने देखी है वो पेशानी[13], वो रुख़्सार[14], वो होंट
ज़िन्दगी जिनके तसव्वुर[15] में लुटा दी हमने
तुझ पे उट्ठी हैं वो खोई हुई साहिर[16] आंखें
तुझ को मालूम है क्यों उम्र गंवा दी हमने

→

Aa ki wabasta hain us husan ki yaaden tujh se
jisne is dil ko parikhana bana rakha tha
Jiski ulphat mein bhula rakhi thi duniya humne
dehar ko dehar ko afsana bana rakha tha
Aashna hain tere kadmon se woh rahen jin per
uski madhosh jawani ne inayat ki hai
Karvan guzare hain jin se usi ra' nai ke
jiski in aankhon ne besood ibadat ki hai
Tujhse kheli hain woh mehboob hawaen jinme
uske malboose ki afsurda mehak baki hai
Tujh pe bhi barsa hai us baam se mehtaab ka noor
Jisme beeti hui raton ki kasak baaki hai
Tune dekhi hai wo peshani, who rukhsar, who hont
zindagi jinke tasavur mein luta di humne
Tujh pe utthi woh khoi hui sahir aankhen
tujh ko maloom hai kyon umre ganwa di humne

To the Rival 

Come, for with you are associated the memories of
that beauteous one
Who had turned this heart into a fairies' abode

In whose love, I had forgotten everything around
And the world had lost all meaning for me;

Associated with you are the pathways
By her youth in drunken pride frequented,

The pathways her beauty's peagant trod,
And my worshipful eyes unsatiated watched;

You too have known the balmy breezes
Soaked in the fragrance of her dress,
Of which only a sad memory remains;

On you too, has rained from that terrace
The moonlight which retains till today the anguish
of the nights, past,

You too have seen the cheeks, the forehead and the
lips
You too have known the spell-binding eyes
Longing for which I have lost a lifetime →

---

1. संबद्ध 2. परियों का घर 3. संसार को 4. परिचित 5. छटा 6. व्यर्थ 7. प्रिय 8. लिबास की 9. उदास 10. छत से 11. चांद का 12. प्रकाश 13. माथा 14. कपोल 15. कल्पना 16. जादूगर

हम पे मुश्तरिका[1] हैं एहसान ग़मे-उल्फ़त के[2]
इतने एहसान कि गिनवाऊं तो गिनवा न सकूं
हमने इस इश्क़ में क्या खोया है क्या सीखा है
जुज़ तेरे[3] और को समझाऊं तो समझा न सकूं

आजिज़ी[4] सीखी, गरीबों की हिमायत सीखी,
यासो-हिर्मान के[5], दुख-दर्द के माने सीखे
ज़ेरदस्तों के[6] मुसाइब को[7] समझना सीखा,
सर्द आहों के, रुख़े-ज़र्द के[8] माने सीखे

जब कहीं बैठ के रोते हैं वो बेकस जिनके
अश्क आंखों में बिलकते हुए सो जाते हैं
नातुवानों के[9] निवालों पे झपटते हैं उक़ाब[10]
बाज़ू तोले हुए मंडलाते हुए आते हैं

जब कभी बिकता है बाज़ार में मज़दूर का गोश्त
शाहराहों पे[11] ग़रीबों का लहू बहता है
आग-सी सीने में रह-रह के उबलती है, न पूछ
अपने दिल पे मुझे क़ाबू ही नहीं रहता है

Hum pe mushtrika hain ahsaan ghame-ulphat ke
itne ahsaan ki ginwaun to ginva ne sakun
humne is ishq mein kya khoya hai kay sikha hai
juz tere aur ko samjhaun to samjha ne sakun

Aajizi sikhi gharibon ki himayat sikhi
yaso-hirmaan ke, dukh-dard ke maane sikhe
zaidasto ke musaib ko samajhna sikha
sard aahon ke, rukhe-zard ke maane sikhe

Jab kahin baith ke rote hain woh bekas jinke
ashq aankhon mein bilakte hue so jaate hain
naatuvano ke nivalon pe jhapatey hain uqaab
baazu tole hue mandlate hue aate hain

Jab kabhi bikta hai bazar mein mazdoor ka gosht
saahrahon pe gharibon ka lahoo behta hai
aag-si seen mein reh-reh ke ubalti hai, ne puchh
apne dil pe mujhe kabu hi nahin rehta hai

The two of us have in common, gifts of love's anguish
So many, that I have lost count of them
But what we have learnt in that love
No one except you will understand :

I have learnt humility, learnt to empathise with the poor,
Learnt the meaning of helplessness, sorrow and despair,
Understood the misery of the oppressed
And felt for myself what sighs and frustration mean...

So that whenever now I see those who crouch and cry
Till the very tears dry up in their eyes,
See those whose morsels are snatched away
By the marauding vultures hovering around,

Whenever the workers' flesh is put on sale
And the blood of the poor on thoroughfare flows—
A fire within me blazes and I am so much wrought
That I completely lose control over my heart.

---

1. साझे 2. प्रेम के दुःखों के 3. तेरे सिवा 4. विनय 5. निराशाओं के 6. असहाय प्राणियों के 7. दुःखों को 8. पीले चेहरे के 9. दुर्बलों के 10. बाज़ 11. राजमार्गों पर

मेरे हमदम, मेरे दोस्त

गर मुझे इसका यक़ीं हो, मेरे हमदम, मेरे दोस्त!
गर मुझे इसका यक़ीं हो कि तेरे दिल की थकन
तेरी आंखों की उदासी, तेरी सीने की जलन
मेरी दिल-जोई, मेरे प्यार से मिट जायेगी
गर मेरा हर्फ़े-तसल्ली[1] वो दवा हो जिस से
जी उठे फिर तेरा उजड़ा हुआ बेनूर दिमाग़
तेरी पेशानी से धुल जायें ये तज़लील के[2] दाग़
तेरी बीमार जवानी को शिफ़ा[3] हो जाये
गर मुझे इसका यक़ीं हो, मेरे हमदम मेरे दोस्त!
मैं तुझे भींच लूं सीने से लगा लूं तुझ को
रोज़ो-शब[4], शामो-सहर[5] मैं तुझे बहलाता रहूं
मैं तुझे गीत सुनाता रहूं हल्के, शीरीं
आबशारों के[6], बहारों के, चमन-ज़ारों के[7] गीत
आमदे-सुबह के[8], महताब के[9], सय्यारों के[10] गीत
तुझसे मैं हुस्नो-मोहब्बत की हिकायात[11] कहूं
कैसे मग़रूर हसीनाओं के बर्फ़ाब से जिस्म
गर्म हाथों की हरारत में[12] पिघल जाते हैं

→

Gar Mujhe iska yakin ho, mere humdum, mere dost !
Gar mujhe iska yakin ho ki tere dil ki thakan
teri aankhon ki udasi, tere seene ki jalan
meri dil-joi, mere pyar se mit jayegi
gar mera hurfe-tasalli woh dawa ho jis se
ji uthe phir tera ujra hua benoor dimagh
teri peshani se dhul jayen ye tazleel ke daag
teri bimar jawani ko shipha ho jaye
Gar Mujhe iska yakin ho, mere humdum, mere dost !
Main tujhe bhinch loon seene se laga loon tujh ko
rozo-shab, shamo-sahar main tujhe behlata rahun
main tujhe geet sunata rahun halke, sheereen
aabsharon ke, baharon ke, chaman-zaaron ke geet
aamde-subah ke, mehtaab ke, sayyaron ke geet
tujhse main husno-mohabbat ki hikayaat kahoon
kaise magroor hasinaon ke barfab se jism
garam hathon ki hararat mein pighal jaate hain

My Comrade, my Friend

If I were sure of it, my comrade, my friend
That the sadness in your eyes, the sickness of your heart
And discomfort in the chest
Can be cured by my affection, my love,
If I were sure that my comforting word
Is the anodyne that will light up your desolate mind
And will bring back your lost pride,
And your sickly youth will bloom again,
If I were sure of it, my comrade my friend,
I would hug you to my heart,
And morning and evening, entertain you
With songs soft and sweet,
The songs of spring, the garden songs and the songs of waterfalls,
Songs of dawn, songs of moonlight and stars,
I would keep telling you tales of love and beauty:
How the cold and haughty beauties melt with the mere touch of a warm hand,

→

1. ढारस का शब्द 2. अपमान के 3. स्वास्थ्य 4. दिन-रात 5. सुबह-शाम 6. झरनों के 7. बागों के 8. प्रातःकाल के 9. चांद के 10. नक्षत्रों के 11. कहानियां 12. गर्मी में

कैसे इक चेहरे के ठहरे हुए मानूस नुक़ूश[1]
देखते-देखते यकलख़्त[2] बदल जाते हैं
किस तरह आरिज़े-महबूब का[3] शफ़्फ़ाक़ बिलूर[4]
यक-ब-यक बादा-ए-अहमर से[5] दहक जाता है
कैसे गुलचीं के[6] लिए झुकती है ख़ुद शाख़े-गुलाब[7]
किस तरह रात का ऐवान[8] महक जाता है
यूं ही गाता रहूं, गाता रहूं, तेरी ख़ातिर
गीत बुनता रहूं, बैठा रहूं, तेरी ख़ातिर
पर मेरे गीत तेरे दुख का मदाबा[9] तो नहीं
नग़मा-ए जर्राह[10] नहीं, मूनिसो-ग़मख़्वाह[11] सही
गीत नश्तर तो नहीं, मरहमे-ग़मख़्वाह[12] सही
तेरे आज़ार[13] का चारा नहीं नश्तर के सिवा
और ये सफ़्फ़ाक मसीहा[14] मेरे क़ब्ज़े में नहीं
इस जहां के किसी ज़ो-रूह के[15] क़ब्जे में नहीं
हां मगर तेरे सिवा, तेरे सिवा, तेरे सिवा!

Kaise ik chehre ke thehre hue manoose nukush
dekhte-dekhte yaklakht badal jaate hain
Kis tarah aarizey-mehboob ka shaffaq billor
yak-b-yak baada-e-ahmar se dehak jaata hai
Kaise gulchin ke liye jhukti hai khud shakhe-gulab
kis tarah raat ka aevaan mahak jaata hai
Yun hi gata rahun, gata rahun, teri khatir
geet bunta rahun, baitha rahun, teri khatir
Par mere geet tere dukh ka madaba to nahin
nagama-e zarraah nahin, muniso-ghamkhwah sahi
Geet nashtar to nahin, marhame-ghamkhwar sahi
mere aazaar ka chara nahin nashtar ke siva
Aur yeh shaffaq masiha mere kabze mein nahin
is jahan ke kisi zo-rooh ke kabze mein nahin
Haan magar tere siva, tere siva, tere siva!

How the familiar furrows on a face suddenly disappear
How the glass-like cheeks of the beloved glow,
How on its own the rose-bough bends before the
flower-picker
And how the night gets soaked in fragrance,
I would keep writing songs for you, keep singing
for your sake;
But my songs are no cure for your sorrow;
They may give solace, but can perform no surgical
operation
And there is no cure of your ill except ruthless
surgery
And I am not such a surgeon,
In fact, nobody else in the world is
Except you, except you and you alone.

---

1 परिचित नैन-नक्श 2. एकाएक 3. प्रेयसी के कपोलों का 4. स्वच्छ कांच 5. शराब की लाली से 6. फूल चुनने वाले के 7. गुलाब की शाखा 8. महल 9. इलाज 10. शल्य-चिकित्सक 11. हमदर्द 12. दुःख-रूपी घाव का मरहम 13. रोग 14. निर्दयी चिकित्सक 15. प्राणी के

ज़िंदां की एक शाम

शाम के पेचो-ख़म[1] सितारों से
ज़ीना-ज़ीना उतर रही है रात
यूं सबा पास से गुज़रती है
जैसे कह दी किसी ने प्यार की बात

सहने-ज़िंदां के बेवतन अश्जार[2]
सरनगू[3] हैं, महव हैं बनाने में

दामने-आसमां पे नक़शो-निगार[4]
शाना-ए-बाम[5] पर दमकता है

महरबां चांदनी का दस्ते-जमील[6]
खाक़ में घुल गयी है आबे-नजूम[7]

नूर में घुल गया है अर्श[8] का नील
सब्ज़ गोशों में नीलगू साये →

Sham ke pecho-kham sitaron se
zina-zina utar rahi hai raat

Yoon saba pas se guzarti hai
jaise keh di kisi ne pyar ki baat

Sehne-zindaan ke bevatan ashjaar
sarnag hain, mehav hain banane mein

Daamne-asmaan pe naksho-nigaar
shaana-e-baam per damakta hai

Meharban chandni ka daste-jameel
khaaq mein ghul gayi hai aabe-najoom

Noor mein ghul gaya hai arsh ka neel
sabz goshon mein neelgoo saye

---

1. उलझे हुए 2. पेड़ 3. नतमस्तक 4. बेल-बूटे 5. छत मुंडेर 6. सुंदर हाथ 7. सितारों की रोशनी 8. आसमां

Prison—One Evening

Step by step the night is descending
Through the zigzag pathway of the stars,

The breeze so blows across
As if it were making an amorous pass,

The homeless trees in the prison compound
With their heads down, are busy

Painting the sky after their heart.
Benign moonlight's lovely hand

Is resting on the terrace's shoulder
The starlight is with dust blended

Like the blue of the sky blending with moonlight. The
blue light falls on the greenery below

→

लहलहाते हैं जिस तरह दिल में
मौजे-दर्दे फ़िराके-यार आये

दिल से पैहम[1] *खयाल कहता है*
इतनी शीरीं[2] *है ज़िदंगी इस पल*

ज़ुल्म का ज़हर घोलने वाले
कामरां[3] *हो सकेंगे आज न कल*

जलवागाहे-विसाल[4] *की शम्में*
वो बुझा भी चुके अगर तो क्या

चांद को गुल करें तो हम जानें।

Lahlahate hain jis tarah dil mein
mauje-darde phiraqe-yaar aaye

Dil se paihum khyal kehta hai
itnee shireen hai zindagi is pal

Zulm ka zehar gholne wale
kamraan ho sakenge aaj na kal

Jalwagahe-visaal ki shammen
woh bujha bhi chuke agar to kya

Chand ko gul karen to hum janen

---

1. लगातार 2. मीठी (हसीन) 3. विजयी 4. मिलन

Like the pangs of separation from the friend
Flitting through the heart

In this lovely night, at such a time
The thought has always crossed my mind

That those who are busy spreading poison
Have never succeeded, nor will they ever succeed.

They may have succeeded in blowing out the candle
In lovers' luminous chambers,

But can they ever blow out the moon?

रंग पैराहन का[1], ख़ुशबू ज़ुल्फ़ लहराने का नाम
मौसमे-गुल[2] है तुम्हारे बाम पर[3] आने का नाम

दोस्तो, उस चश्मो-लब की[4], कुछ कहो जिसके बग़ैर
गुलिस्तां की बात रंगीं[5] है, न मैख़ाने का नाम

फिर नज़र में फूल महके, दिल में फिर शम्एं जलीं
फिर तसव्वुर ने[6] लिया उस बज़्म में जाने का नाम

अब किसी लैला को भी इक़रारे-महबूबी[7] नहीं
इन दिनों बदनाम है हर एक दीवाने का नाम

हम से कहते हैं चमन वाले, ग़रीबाने-चमन[8]
तुम कोई अच्छा-सा रख लो अपने वीराने का नाम

Rang pairahan ka khushboo zulf lehrane ka naam
mausame-gul hai tumhare baam par aane ka naam

Dosto, us chashmo-lab ki, kuchh kaho jiske bagair
gulistan ki baat rangin hai, na maikhane ka naam

Phir nazar mein phool mehke, dil me phir shamein jalin
phir tasavur ne liya us bazm mein jaane ka naam

Ab kisi laila ko bhi iqrarey-mehboobi nahin
in dino badnaam hai har ek diwane ka naam

Hum se kehte hain chaman wale, gharibane-chaman
tum koi achha-sa rakh lo apne veerane ka naam

---

1. लिबास का 2. वसन्त ऋतु 3. छत पर 4. आंखों और होठों की 5. रंगीन 6. कल्पना ने 7. प्रेमिका होने का इक़रार 8. प्रवासी

The true colour is the colour of your dress, and
fragrance, the fragrance from your hair, floating
The spring comes only with you on the terrace
coming.

O friends, say something about those lips and eyes
Without which all talk of the garden is dull, and the
tavern desolate lies

Again, the flowers bloom before the eyes, again the
heart is glowing
Again, I fancy myself to her gathering going

Notoriety is dogging every lover around
No Laila, these days, is willing to be in love, bound

We, who are exiled from it, are advised by the
residents of the garden:
You should give some attractive name to your place
of desolation.

न तुम आए हो न शबे-इन्तिज़ार[1] गुज़री है
तलाश में है सहर[2], बार-बार गुज़री है

जुनूं में[3] जितनी भी गुज़री ब-कार[4] गुज़री है
अगरचे दिल पे ख़राबी हज़ार गुज़री है

हुई है हज़रते-नासेह से[5] गुफ्तगू जिस शब
वो शब ज़रूर सरे-कू-ए-यार[6] गुज़री है

वो बात सारे फ़साने में[7] जिसका ज़िक्र न था
वो बात उनको बहुत नागवार गुज़री है

न गुल खिले हैं, न उनसे मिले, न मय पी है
अजीब रंग में अब के बहार गुज़री है

चमन पे ग़ारते-गुलचीं से[8] जाने क्या गुज़री
क़फ़स से[9] आज सबा[10] बेक़रार गुज़री है

(जेल में लिखी ग़ज़ल)

Na tum aaye ho na shabe-intezaar guzri hai
talash mein hai sehar, baar-baar guzri hai

Junoon mein jitnee bhi guzri b-kaar guzri hai
agarche dil pe kharabi hazaar guzri hai

Hui hai hazrate-naaseh se guftagoo jis shab
woh shab zaroor sare-ku-e-yaar guzri hai

Woh baat saare phasane mein jiska zikra na tha
woh baat unko bahut nagawar guzri hai

Na gul khile hain, na unse miley, na may pi hai
ajeeb rang mein ab ke bahaar guzri hai

Chaman pe gaarte-gulchin se jaane kya guzri
qafas se aaj saba beqarar guzri hai

---

1. इन्तिज़ार की रात 2. सुबह 3. उन्माद में 4. काम में 5. उपदेशक से 6. प्रेमिका की गली में 7. कहानी में 8. माली की लूट-खसोट से 9. पिंजरे से 10. प्रभात-समीर

Neither have you come, nor has the night of waiting
passed
The dawn is hovering around, and has repeatedly
for you asked

The time spent in frenzy is indeed well spent
Although the heart has with suffering bent

Whenever I have discoursed with the preacher,
invariably
I have spent the night in my beloved's alley

That which was never a part of the story
That bit has piqued him immensely

Neither have the flowers blossomed, nor have I met
her, not drunk wine
How strangely has the spring season passed this
time!

God knows how fared the garden in the wake of
pillage by the gardener
This morning, the breeze has very restlessly passed
across the cage, here

मौज़ू-ए-सुख़न

गुल हुई जाती है[1] अफ़सुर्दा[2] सुलगती हुई शाम
धुल के निकलेगी अभी चश्म-ए-महताब से[3] रात
और मुश्ताक़ निगाहों से सुनी जाएगी
और उन हाथों से मस[4] होंगे ये तरसे हुए हाथ

उनका आंचल है कि रुख़्सार[5] कि पैराहन[6] है
कुछ तो है जिससे हुई जाती है चिलमन रंगीं
जाने उस ज़ुल्फ़ की मौहूम[7] घनी छांव में
टिमटिमाता है वो आवेज़ा[8] अभी तक कि नहीं

आज फिर हुस्ने-दिलारा की[9] वही धज होगी
वही ख़्वाबीदा-सी[10] आंखें, वही काजल की लकीर
रंगे-रुख़्सार पे[11] हल्का-सा वो ग़ाज़े का गुबार
संदली हाथ पे धुंधली-सी हिना की[12] तहरीर[13] →

Gul hui jaati hai afsurda sulagti hui shaam
dhul ke niklegi abhi chashm-e-mehtaab se raat
aur mushtaq nigahon se suni jayegi
aur un hathon se mas honge ye tarse hue haath

Unka anchal hai ki rukhasar ki pairahan hai
kuchh to hai jisse hui jaati hai chilman rangin
jaane us zulph ki mohoom ghani chhaon mein
timtimata hai woh aaveza abhi tak ki nahin

Aaj phir husne-dilara ki wahi dhaj hogi
wahi khwabida-si aankhen, wahi kajal ki lakir
range-rukhsaar pe halka-sa woh ghaze ka gubaar
sandali haath pe dhundhli-si hina ki tehreer

---

1. बुझ रही है 2. उदास 3. चांद के चश्मे से 4. स्पर्श 5. कपोल 6. लिबास 7. धुंधली 8. कान का बुंदा 9. मनमोहक सौन्दर्य की 10. स्वप्निल-सी 11. कपोलों के रंग पर 12. मेहंदी की 13. लिखाई, चित्रकारी

The Subject of Poetry

The evening, sad and russet, is setting fast
And soon, the night, bathed in the springs of the moon, will burst forth
My eyes will have their wish fulfilled
While my longing hand will hold her hand.

Her fringed veil, her face or her dress...
Some such thing is lending a glow to the parting curtain already,
And I wonder if that ear-ring dances
Under the deep shadow of her hair still!

Those sleepy eyes with penciled lids,
A little dash of rouge upon the glowing cheek,
And that hand with a delicate touch of mehndi—
Surely, her beauty will be visited again...

→

अपने अफ़कार की[1], अशआर की[2] दुनिया है यही
जाने-मज़मूं[3] है यही, शाहिदे-माने[4] है यही

आज तक सुर्ख़ों-सियाह सदियों के साये के तले
आदमो-हव्वा की औलाद पे[5] क्या गुज़री है
मौत और ज़ीस्त[6] की रोज़ाना सफ़ूआराई में[7]
हम पे क्या गुज़रेगी, अजदाद पे[8] क्या गुज़री है

इन दमकते हुए शहरों की फ़रावां[9] मख़्लूक़[10]
क्यों फ़क़त मरने की हसरत में जिया करती है
ये हसीं खेत, फटा पड़ता है जोबन जिनका
किस लिए इनमें फ़क़त भूक उगा करती है →

Apne aphkar ki, ashaar ki duniya hai yahi
jaane-mazmoo hai yahi, shahide-maane hai yahi

Aaj tak surkho-siyaah sadiyon ke saye ke tale
aadmo-haova ki aulaad pe kya guzri hai
maut aur zist ki rozana saphaarai mein
hum pe kya guzregi ajdaad pe kya guzri hai

In damakte hue shehron ki pharawa makhlooq
kyon phakat marne ki hasrat mein jiya karti hai
ye hasin khet, phata parta hai joban jinka
kis liye inmen phakat bhook uga karti hai

---

1. विचारों की 2. शे'रों की 3. विषय की जान 4. अर्थों की सुन्दरता 5. सन्तान पर 6. जीवन 7. मोर्चेबंदी में 8. पुरखों पर 9. प्रचुर 10. जनता

This is the realm of my imagining, the subject of my poetry
And all my meaning inheres in it only.

Under the shadow of dark and bloody centuries
How have the children of Adam and Eve fared,
In the tussle between life and death everyday
How are we coping, how our ancestors lived,

Why the people in these swarming, bright cities
Live only in the fond hope of death,
Why the fields bursting forth with lovely shoots
Produce only hunger?

→

ये हर इक सम्त[1] पुरअसरार[2] कड़ी दीवारें
जल बुझे जिन में हज़ारों की जवानी के चिराग़
ये हर इक गाम पे[3] उन ख़्वाबों की मक़्तल-गाहें[4]
जिनके परतौ से[5] चिराग़ां[6] हैं हज़ारों के दिमाग़

ये भी हैं ऐसे कई और भी मज़मूं[7] होंगे
लेकिन उस शोख़ के आहिस्ता से खुलते हुए होंट
हाय उस जिस्म के कम्बख़्त दिलावेज़ ख़ुतूत[8]
आप ही कहिए कहीं ऐसे भी अफ़सूं[9] होंगे

अपना मौज़ू-ए-सुख़न इनके सिवा और नहीं
तबए-शायर का[10] वतन इनके सिवा और नहीं

Ye har ik samt purasraar kari diwaren
jal bujhe jin mein hazaron ki jawani ke chirag
ye har ik gaam pe un khwabon ki maqtal-gaahen
jinke partau se chinraga hain hazaron ke dimaag

Ye bhi hain aise kai aur bhi mazmoo honge
lekin us shokh ke aahista se khulte hue hont
haye us jism ke kambakht dilavez khutoot
aap hi kahiye kahin aise bhi aphsoon honge

Apna maujoo-e-sukhan inke siva aur nahin
tabe-shayar ka vatan inke siva aur nahin

---

1. ओर 2. रहस्यपूर्ण 3. पग पर 4. वध-स्थल 5. प्रतिबिम्ब से 6. दीप्तिमान 7. विषय 8. हृदयाकर्षक रेखाएं (बनावट) 9. जादू 10. शायर की प्रकृति

On every side stand high walls on constant guard
Behind which is buried the youth of countless men
and women,
On every side are seen the burial ground of dreams
That illumin the minds of millions till today...

These are, and there must be many such subjects
more...
But her softly opening lips
And her body's bewitching curves
Work a magic unbelievable...

They are the subject of my verse,
The haunts of a poet's mind,
And nothing else.

बोल...

बोल कि लब आज़ाद हैं तेरे
बोल, ज़बां अब तक तेरी है
तेरा सुतवां[1] जिस्म है तेरा
बोल कि जां अब तक तेरी है

देख कि आहनगर की[2] दुकां में
तुन्द[3] हैं शोले, सुर्ख़ है आहन[4]
खुलने लगे क़ुफ़लों के[5] दहाने[6]
फैला हर ज़ंजीर का दामन

बोल, ये थोड़ा वक़्त बहुत है
जिस्मो-ज़बां की मौत से पहले
बोल कि सच ज़िंदा है अब तक
बोल कि जो कहना है कह ले

Bol ki lab azaad hain tere
bol, zaban ab tak teri hai
tera sutvan jism hai tera
bol ki jaan ab tak teri hai

Dekh ki aahnagar ki dukan mein
tund hain sholey, surkh hai aahan
khulne lage kuphlon ke dahane
faila har zanjeer ka daaman

Bol, ye thoda waqt bahut hai
jismo-zaban ki maut se pahle
bol ki such zinda hai ab tak
bol ki jo kehna hai keh le

---

1. तना हुआ 2. लोहार की 3. तेज़ 4. लोहा 5. तालों के 6. मुंह

Speak up

Speak up, for you are free to speak
Speak up, for as yet you are master of your tongue
Your sturdy body is as yet your own,
Speak up, for there is life in the body still.

See the flames leaping up
See the red iron hot
See the lock opening and chains loosening
At the blacksmith's shop.

Speak up, for the little time you have is a lot,
Speak up, let the whole truth come out,
Before the body dies and life ebbs away
Speak you up and say what you have to say.

सियासी लीडर से

सालहासाल से[1] ये बेआसरा जकड़े हुए हाथ
रात के सख़्त सियाह सीने में पैवस्त[2] रहे
जिस तरह तिनका समंदर में हो सरगर्मे-सफ़र
जिस तरह तीतरी कोहसार[3] में यलगार [4] करे!

और अब रात के संगीन वसीह[5] सीने में
इतने घाव हैं कि जिस सिम्त[6] नज़र जाती है
जा-बजा नूर[7] का इक जाल-सा बुन रक्खा है
दूर से सुबह के धड़कने की सदा आती है

तेरा सरमाया, तेरी आस यही हाथ तो हैं
और कुछ भी तो नहीं पास, यही हाथ तो हैं
तुझको मंज़ूर नहीं ग़लबा-ए-ज़ुल्मत[8] लेकिन
तुझको मंज़ूर है ये हाथ कलम हो जायें[9]
और मशरक के कमीगह[10] में धड़कता हुआ दिन
रात की आहनी[11] मैय्यत के तले दब जाये।

Saal-ha-saal se ye beaasra jakre hue haath
raat ke sakht siyah seen mein pevast rahe
Jis tarah tinka samandar mein ho sargarme-safar
jis tarah titari kohsaar mein yalgaar kare!

Aur ab raat ke sangeen vasih seene mein
itne ghav hain ki jis simt nazar jaati hai
Jaa-baza noor ka ik jaal-sa bun rakha hai
door se subah ke dharakne ki sada aati hai

Tera sarmaya, teri aas yahi haath to hain
aur kuchh bhi to nahin paas yahi haath to hain
Tujhko manzoor nahin ghalba-e-zulmat lekin
Tujhko manzoor hai yeh haath kalam ho jayen
aur mashrak ke kamigah mein dharakta hua din
raat ki aahni maiyyat ke tale dab jaye

---

1. बरसों से 2. धंसे हुए 3. पहाड़ 4. चीखना 5. लंबा-चौड़ा 6. दिशा 7. प्रकाश 8. अंधेरे का साम्राज्य 9. कट जायें 10. ठिकाना 11. भारी

To the Political Leader

Like a straw, struggling against a torrent of the ocean
Like a butterfly flapping its wings against the
mountain-side,
For years, these helpless hands have been
Tearing at the dark and heavy bosom of the night;

And now so many wounds appear
On this bosom that on whichever side you look
You see a mesh woven by light

And hear a distinct sound of the pulsating dawn.
These hands are your only asset
You surely don't want them to be overwhelmed by
darkness,
Can you then surrender these hands
And allow the dawn, pulsating in the east
To be buried under the heavy weight of night ?

आज तन्हाई किसी हमदमे[1] देरीं की तरह
करने आई है मेरी साक़ीगिरी शाम ढले
मुन्तज़िर[2] बैठे हैं हम दोनों कि महताब[3] उभरे
और तेरा अक़्स ढलकने लगे हर साये के तले

Aaj tanhai kisi humdame derin ki tarah
karne aai hai meri saqigiri shaam dhale
muntazir baithen hain hum dono ki mehtaab ubhre
aur tera aqs dhalakane lage her saaye ke tale

1. पुराना दोस्त 2. इन्तज़ार में 3. चांद

Like a long-lost friend, loneliness, this evening
Has come to act as my Saqi
We are both waiting for the moon to rise
So that under every shade your face we can see

दर्द आयेगा दबे पाँव

और कुछ देर में, जब फिर मेरे तन्हा दिल को
फ़िक्र आ लेगी कि तन्हाई का क्या चारा करे
दर्द आयेगा दबे पांव, लिए सुर्ख़ चिराग़
वो जो इक दर्द धड़कता है कहीं दिल से परे

शो'लाए-दर्द जो पहलू में लपक उट्ठेगा
दिल की दीवार पे हर नक़्श[1] दमक उट्ठेगा

हल्क़ाए-ज़ुल्फ़[2] कहीं, गोशए-रुख़्सार[3] कहीं
हिज्र का दश्त[4] कहीं, गुलशने-दीदार[5] कहीं

लुत्फ़ की बात कहीं, प्यार का इक़रार कहीं
दिल से फिर होगी मेरी बात कि ऐ दिल, ऐ दिल

ये जो महबूब बना है तेरी तन्हाई का
ये तो मेहमां है घड़ी भर का, चला जायेगा

इससे कब तेरी मुसीबत का मदावा[6] होगा

→

Aur kuchh der mein, jab phir mere tanha dil ko
phikra aa legi ki tanhai ka kya chara kare
dard aayega dabe paon, liye surkh chirag
woh jo ik dard dharakta hai kahin dil se pare

Sholai-dard jo pehloo mein lapak utthega
dil ki diwar pe har naqsh damak utthega

Halkae-zulph kahin, goshae-rukhsar kahin
hizra ka dasht kahin, gulshan-e-didaar kahin

Lutph ki baat kahin, pyar ka iqraar kahin
dil se phir hogi meri baat ki ae dil, ae dil

Ye jo mehboob bana hai teri tanhai ka
ye to mehmaan hai ghari bhar ka, chala jayega

Isse kab teri musibat ka madava hoga

---

1. चित्र 2. केशों के बल 3. कपोलों का कोण 4. जंगल 5. दर्शन रूपी बाग 6. इलाज

Pain will Come Soft-footed

In a little while when my lonesome heart will be
worried
As to how this loneliness will pass,
A pain that throbs around the heart
Will come lightfooted carrying a red candle in hand.

The flaming pain will leap up in the side
And many a picture will reflect on the heart's wall...

The picture of the curl, the picture of the cheek
The picture of desolate separation, picture of the
flowery sight of union,

Some moment of joy, some memory of love...
And then I will say to my heart

This companion of my loneliness
Is a guest who will soon depart,

Moreover, for your problem, it has no solution.

→

मुश्तइल होके अभी उट्ठेंगे वहशी साये
ये चला जायेगा, रह जायेंगे बाक़ी साये
रात भर जिनसे तेरा ख़ून-ख़राबा होगा
जंग ठहरी है कोई खेल नहीं है ऐ दिल
दुश्मने-जां हैं सभी, सारे के सारे क़ातिल
ये कड़ी रात भी, ये साये भी, तन्हाई भी
दर्द और जंग में कुछ मेल नहीं है ऐ दिल
लाओ सुलगाओ कोई जोशो-ग़ज़ब का अंगार
तैश की आतिशे-जर्राह कहीं से लाओ
वो दहकता हुआ गुलज़ार कहीं से लाओ
जिसमें गर्मी भी है, हरकत भी, तवानाई भी
हो न हो अपने क़बीले का भी कोई लश्कर
मुन्तज़िर होगा अंधेरे की फ़सीलों के उधर
इनको शो'लों के रजज़ अपना पता तो देंगे
ख़ैर, हम तक वो न पहुंचे भी, सदा तो देंगे
दूर कितनी है अभी सुब्ह, बता तो देंगे

(जेल में लिखी नज़्म)

Mushtail hoke abhi utthenge vehshi saaye
ye chala jayega, reh jayenge baaki saaye
Raat bhar jinse tera khoon-kharaba hoga
jung thehri hai koi khel nahin hai ae dil
Dushmane-jaan hain sabhi, saare ke saare qaatil
ye kari raat bhi, ye saaye bhi, tahai bhi
Dard aur jung mein kuchh mail nahin hai ae dil
Laao sulgao koi josho-ghazab ka angaar
taish ki aatishe-zarrah kahin se laao
Woh dehkta hua gulzaar kahin se laao
jisme garmi bhi hai, harkat bhi, tavanai bhi
Ho na ho apne kabile ka bhi koi lashkar
muntazir hoga andhere ki phasilon ke udhar
Inko sho'lon ki rajaz apna pata to denge
khair, hum tak woh na pahunche bhi, sada to denge
door kitnee hai abhi subah, bata to denge

Fierce shadows will rise again,
The guest will depart and the shadows will remain

And all night, you'll have to grapple with them.
It's a war, no child's play, O heart

These shadows, this loneliness, this night,
Enemies of life, a murderer each one of them.

Pain has no place in war, O heart

Kindle a red, hot flame of wrath,
Mighty, dynamic and steadfast.

May be, some battalion of our tribe
Is waiting on the other side of the rampart dark.

This fiery martial music will at least
Make them aware of our presence here,
They may not be able to reach us,
They will at least call us back
And tell us how far we are still from the dawn.

नौहा

मुझको शिकवा है मेरे भाई कि तुम जाते-जाते
ले गये साथ मेरी उम्रे-गुज़िश्ता[1] की किताब
इसमें तो मेरी बहुत कीमती तस्वीरें थीं

इसमें बचपन था मेरा और मेरा अहदे-शबाब
इसके बदले दे गये मुझे तुम जाते-जाते
अपने ग़म का ये दहकता हुआ ख़ूंरंग गुलाब

क्या करूं भाई ये ऐज़ाज़[2] मैं क्योंकर पहनूं
मुझसे ले लो मेरी सब चाक़ कमीज़ों का हिसाब
आख़री बार अब लो मान लो इक ये भी सवाल
आज तक तुमसे मैं लौटा नहीं मायूसे जवाब

आके ले जाओ तुम अपना ये दहकता हुआ फूल

मुझको लौटा दो मेरी उम्रे-गुज़िश्ता की किताब

Mujhko shikva hai mere bhai ki tum jaate-jaate
le gaye sath meri umre-guzishta ki kitab
ismein to meri bahut kimtee tasveeren thin

Ismein bachpan tha mera aur mera ahde-shbaab
iske badle de gaye mujhe tum jaate-jaate
apne ghum ka ye dehkta hua khoonrang gulab

Kya karoon bhai ye aizaaz main kyonkar pehnoon
mujhse le lo meri sab chaak kameezon ka hisaab
akhri baar ab lo maan lo ik ye bhi sawal
aaj tak tumse main lauta nahin mayuse jawab

aake le jao tum apna ye dehkta hua phool

Mujhko lauta do meri umre-guzishta ki kitab

---

1. बीता समय 2. इनाम

Elegy

I regret, my brother, that with you at the time of departure
You took away my album of past years—
This album had priceless pictures of my childhood and youth—

And in lieu of it, you left with me
A blood red rose of your scalding grief;
What do I do of it ? Where do I go wearing this award ?

Here, take this account of shirts already lost.
You have never turned me back disappointed till today
Pray, grant this lost wish too :
Come, and take away your flaming flower
And give me back my book of life, gone with you

शामे-फ़िराक़[1] अब न पूछ, आई और आके टल गई
दिल था कि फिर बहल गया, जां थी कि फिर संभल गई

बज़्मे-ख़याल में[2] तेरे हुस्न की शम्अ जल गई
दर्द का चांद बुझ गया, हिज्र की[3] रात ढल गई

जब तुझे याद कर लिया, सुबह महक-महक उठी
जब तेरा ग़म जगा लिया, रात मचल-मचल गई

दिल से तो हर मुआमला करके चले थे साफ़ हम
कहने में उनके सामने बात बदल-बदल गई

आख़िरे-शब के[4] हमसफ़र 'फ़ैज़' न जाने क्या हुए
रह गई किस जगह सबा[5], सुबह किधर निकल गई

(जेल में लिखी नज़्म)

Shaame-firaq ab na puchh, aai aur aake tal gai
dil tha ki phir behal gaya, jaan thi ki phir sambhal gai

Bazme-khyaal mein tere husn ki shamae jal gai
dard ka chand bujh gaya, hizra ki raat dhal gai

Jab tujhe yaad kar liya, subah mehak-mehak uthi
jab tera ghum jaga liya, raat machal-machal gai

Dil se to har muaamla karke chale the saaf hum
kehne mein unke saamne baat badal-badal gai

Aakhire-shab ke humsafar 'Faiz' na jaane kya hue
reh gai kis jagah sabaa, subah kidhar nikal gai

---

1. वियोग की शाम या रात 2. कल्पनाओं की सभा में 3. वियोग की 4. रात के अन्त में 5. प्रभात-समीर

O ask me not how I passed the evening of separation
The heart somehow its poise regained, the life
somehow resumed its normal motion

The realm of thought got illuminated by your beauty
The pain evaporated withal and the night of
separation ceased to be

Whenever I remembered you the morning became
redolent
And whenever your sorrow I recalled the night into
a toss went

I had left home with complete clarity as to what
I would say
But in her presence, my words went into disarray

I know not, Faiz, what happened to my companions
of last night
Which way the breeze went, where to the morning
took flight

शैख़ साहब से रस्मो-राह न की
शुक्र है ज़िन्दगी तबाह न की

तुझ को देखा तो सीर-ए-चश्म हुए[1]
तुझ को चाहा तो और चाह न की

थे शबे-हिज्र[2] *काम और बहुत*
हमने फ़िक्रे-दिले-तबाह न की

कौन क़ातिल बचा है शहर में 'फ़ैज़'
जिससे यारों ने रस्मो-राह न की

Shaikh sahab se rasmo-rah na ki
shukra hai zindagi tabaah na ki

Tujh ko dekha to ser-chashm hue
tujh ko chaha to aur chaah na ki

Thi shabe-hizre kaam aur bahut
humne phikre-dile-tabaah na ki

Kaun qaatil bacha hai shehar mein 'Faiz'
jis se yaaron ne rasmo-raah na ki

---

1. आंखों की सारी भूख मिट गई 2. वियोग की रात

I never made friends with Monsieur, preacher
Thank God, I did not ruin my life for ever

Your sight was for the eyes a feast entire
When I loved you, I had no other desire

On the night of separation, we had to work a lot
So we cared not for our ruined heart

Which murderer, O Faiz, is in the city remaining
With whom our friends don't have understanding

मुझसे पहली-सी मोहब्बत मेरे महबूब न मांग

मुझसे पहली सी मोहब्बत मेरे महबूब न मांग !

मैंने समझा था कि तू है तो दरख़्शां[1] है हयात[2]
तेरा ग़म है तो ग़मे-दह्र का[3] झगड़ा क्या है
तेरी सूरत से है आलम में[4] बहारों को सबात[5]
तेरी आंखों के सिवा दुनिया में रक्खा क्या है

तू जो मिल जाए तो तक़दीर निगू हो जाए[6]
यूं न था, मैंने फ़कत[7] चाहा था यूं हो जाए
और भी दुख हैं ज़माने में मोहब्बत के सिवा
राहतें[8] और भी हैं वस्ल की[9] राहत के सिवा →

Mujhse pehli si mohabbat mere mehboob na maang !

Maine samjha tha ki tu hai to darkhashan hai hayaat
tera ghum hai to ghume-dehar ka jhagra kya hai
teri surat se hai aalam mein baharon ko sabaat
teri aankhon ke siva duniya mein rakha kya hai

Tu jo mil jaaye to taqdir nigu ho jaaye
yun na tha, maine phaqat chaha tha yun ho jaaye
aur bhi dukh hain zamane mein mohabbat ke siva
raahten aur bhi hain vasl ki raahat ke siva

---

1. प्रकाशमान 2. जीवन 3. सांसारिक चिंताओं का 4. संसार में 5. स्थायित्व 6. सिर झुका ले 7. केवल 8. आनन्द 9. मिलन की।

Ask me not for Love, O dear like Before

Ask me not for love, O dear, like before!

With you around, I had thought, life is all aglow,
When I sorrow for you, I need not bother about
the sufferings of the world,
Your beauty gives permanence to the spring season,
I had thought
That nothing else is worthwhile in the world except
your eyes,

But that is not it;
There are other sorrows too in the world, apart from
the sorrows of love
And other joys besides the joys of union—
→

अनगिनत सदियों के तारीक बहीमाना तिलिस्म[1]
रेशमो-अतलसो-कमख़्वाब के बुनवाये हुए
जा-ब-जा बिकते हुए कूचा-ओ-बाज़ार में जिस्म
ख़ाक में लिथड़े हुए, ख़ून में नहलाये हुए

जिस्म निकले हुए अमराज़ के[2] *तन्नूरों से*
पीप बहती हुई गलते हुए नासूरों से
लौट जाती है उधर को भी नज़र, क्या कीजे
अब भी दिलकश है तेरा हुस्न, मगर क्या कीजे

और भी दुख हैं ज़माने में मोहब्बत के सिवा
राहतें और भी हैं वस्ल की राहत के सिवा

मुझसे पहली सी मोहब्बत मेरी महबूब न मांग !

Anginat sadiyon ke tareek bahimana tilasm
reshmo-atlaso-kamkhwab ke bunvaye hue
jaa-ba-jaa bikte hue kucha-o-bazaar mein zism
khaaq mein lithre hue, khoon mein nehlaye hue

Zism nikle hue amraaz ke tannuron se
peep behti hui galte hue naasuron se
laut jaati hai udhar ko bhi nazar, kya kijey
ab bhi dilkash hai tera husn, magar kya kijey

Aur bhi dukh hain zamane mein mohabbat ke siva
raahtein aur bhi hain vasal ki raahat ke siva

Mujhse pehli si mohabbat meri mehboob ne maang !

---

1. अन्धकारपूर्ण पाशविक जादू 2. रोगों के

A web of brutal darkness woven over centuries,
Human bodies on sale in the street and the market
place,
Bodies bathed in dust and blood,

Diseased bodies with festering wounds—
The eye is arrested by all this, it cannot help;
Your beauty though is as attractive as before

There are other sorrows also in the world beside
the sorrows of love
And other joys apart from the joys of union.

Do not ask me, dear, for love like before.

चन्द रोज़ और मेरी जान

चन्द रोज़ और मेरी जान ! फ़क़त[1] चन्द ही रोज़ !
ज़ुल्म की छांव में दम लेने पै मजबूर हैं हम
और कुछ देर सितम सह लें, तड़प लें, रो लें
अपने अजदाद की[2] मीरास[3] हैं मा'ज़ूर[4] हैं हम
जिस्म पर क़ैद है, जज़्बात पै ज़ंजीरें हैं
फ़िक्र[5] महबूस हैं[6], गुफ़्तार पै[7] ता'ज़ीरें[8] हैं
अपनी हिम्मत है कि हम फिर भी जिये जाते हैं
ज़िन्दगी क्या है किसी मुफ़लिस की क़बा[9] है जिसमें
हर घड़ी दर्द के पेबंद लगे जाते हैं
लेकिन अब ज़ुल्म की मीयाद के दिन थोड़े हैं
इक ज़रा सब्र, कि फ़रियाद के दिन थोड़े हैं →

Chand roz aur meri jaan ! Phaqat chand hi roz !
Zulm ki chhaon mein dum leney pai majboor hain hum
aur kuchh der sitam seh len, tarap len, ro len
apne ajdaad ki miraas hain mazoor hain hum

Jism par qaid hai, jazjbaat pai zanjeerein hain
phikra mehboos hain, guftaar pai ta'zeerein hain

Apni himmat hai ki hum phir bhi jiye jaate hain
zindagi kya hai kisi muphlis ki qaba hai jismein
har ghari dard ke peband lage jaate hain

Lekin ab zulm ki miyaad ke din thore hein
ik zara sabra, ki phariyad ke din thore hain

---

1. केवल 2. पुरखों की 3. बपौती 4. विवश 5. विचार 6. क़ैद में हैं अर्थात् जकड़े हुए हैं 7. बोलने पर 8. प्रतिबंध 9. निर्धन का कुर्ता

A Few Days More, My Love

For only a few days more, my love, only a few days more

We are obliged to live under the shadow of tyranny,
For only a few days more, we have to suffer and sigh
For what our forefathers have bequeathed to us.
Our body is in fetters, our feelings are in chains held,

The mind in bondage, speech under censor—
Our life is but a poor man's apron,
Full of endless patches of agony and pain
And if we are alive, it is only by our grit and courage.
The days of tyranny are however numbered now.
Hold on for a while, for now you do not have to suffer for long.

→

अर्सा-ए-दह्र की[1] झुलसी हुई वीरानी में
हमको रहना है पर यूंही तो नहीं रहना है

अजनबी हाथों का बेनाम गिरांबार सितम[2]
आज सहना है हमेशा तो नहीं सहना है

ये तेरे हुस्न से लिपटी हुई आलाम की[3] गर्द
अपनी दो-रोज़ा जवानी की शिकस्तों का शुमार[4]

चांदनी रातों का बेकार दहकता हुआ दर्द
दिल की बेसूद[5] तड़प, जिस्म की मायूस पुकार

चन्द रोज़ और मेरी जान ! फ़क़त चन्द ही रोज़ !

Arsa-e-dehar ki jhulsi hui veerani mein
humko rehna hai per yunhi to nahin rehna hai

Ajnabi hathon ka benaam giranbaar sitam
aaj sehna hai hamesha to nahin sehna hai

Ye tere husn se liptee hui alaam ki gard
apni do-roza jawani ki shikaston ka shumaar

Chandni raaton ka bekaar dehakta hua dard
dil ki besud tarap, jism ki maayus pukar

Chand roz aur meri jaan ! phaqat chand hi roz !

---

1. संसार-रूपी मैदान की 2. भारी अत्याचार 3. दुःखों की 4. गणना 5. व्यर्थ

In this vast and scortching desert of life
We have to live, but not for ever,

The cruelty of invisible heavy hand
Though we suffer today
Not for ever, do we have to suffer;

Your beauty with sorrow besmeared,
The reverses of my shortlived youth

And the avoidable pangs of separation in moonlit nights,
The heartbreaks, unnecessary pain and despair—

Only a few days more, my love, only a few days more.

दो इश्क़

ताज़ा हैं अभी याद में ऐ साक़ी-ए-गुलफ़ाम[1]
वो अक्से रुख़े-यार से[2] लहके हुए अय्याम[3]
वो फूल-सी खिलती हुई दीदार[4] की साअत[5]
वो दिल-सा धड़कता हुआ उम्मीद का हंगाम[6]

उम्मीद कि लो जागा ग़मे-दिल का नसीबा
लो शौक़ की[7] तरसी हुई शब हो गई आख़िर
लो डूब गये दर्द के बेख़्वाब सितारे
अब चमकेगा बेसब्र निगाहों का मुक़द्दर

इस बाम से निकलेगा तेरे हुस्न का ख़ुरशीद[8]
उस कुंज से फूटेगी किरन रंगे-हिना की[9]
इस दर से[10] बहेगा तेरी रफ़्तार का सीमाब[11]
उस राह पर फूटेगी शफ़क़[12] तेरी क़बा की[13]

वापस नहीं फेरा कोई फ़रमान[14] जुनूं का[15]
तन्हा नहीं लौटी कभी आवाज़ जरस की[16] →

Taza hain abhi yaad mein ae saaqi-e-gulpham
woh akse rukhe-yaar se lehke hue ayyaam
Woh phool-si khilti hui didaar ki saaut
woh dil-sa dharakta hua ummid ka hungaam
Ummid ki lo jaaga ghame-dil ka nasiba
lo shauq ki tarsi hui shab ho gai aakhir
Lo doob gaye dard ke bekhwab sitare
ab chamkega besabra nigahon ka muqaddar
Is baam se niklega tere husn ka khursheed
us kunj se phutegi kiran range-hina ki
Is dar se bahega teri raftaar ka simaab
us raah per phootegi shafaq teri qaba ki
Vapas nahin phera koi pharman junoon ka
tanha nahin lauti kabhi awaaz jaras ki

---

1. फूल जैसा साक़ी 2. प्रेमिका के मुखड़े के प्रतिबिम्ब से 3. दिन (जीवन) 4. दर्शन 5. क्षण 6. समय 7. इश्क की 8. सूरज 9. मेहंदी के रंग की 10. दरवाज़े से 11. पारा 12. सूर्यास्त की लालिमा 13. कुर्ते (लिबास) की 14. आदेश 15. उन्माद का 16. घंटे की

Two Loves

I remember very vividly still, O rose-like Saqi
The days glowing with our beloved's beauty,
The blossom-time of our sight of her
And the hope of meeting her with a throbbing heart,

The hope that the sad heart has at last turned a corner
That our passion is now going to be gratified
That our painful wait and patience are going to be rewarded now

That from this terrace her beauty like the moon will rise
That from that corner its henna-like rays will appear
That from that doorway her steps like quicksilver will flow
And from that pathway her garment like the twilight glow.

Never did I unheed the prompting of passion,
Never did the trumpet unanswered go, →

ख़ैरियते-जां[1], राहते-तन[2], सेहते-दामां[3]
सब भूल गईं मसलहतें अहले-हवस की[4]

इस राह में जो सब पे गुज़रती है वो गुज़री
तन्हा पसे-जिंदां[5], कभी रुसवा सरे-बाज़ार[6]
गरजे हैं बहुत शैख़ सरे-गोशा-ए-मिम्बर[7]
कड़के हैं बहुत अहले-हुकम[8] बर-सरे-दरबार[9]

छोड़ा नहीं ग़ैरों ने कोई नावके-दुश्नाम[10]
छूटी नहीं अपनों से कोई तर्ज़े-मलामत[11]
इस इश्क़ न उस इश्क़ पे नादिम है मगर दिल
हर दाग़ है इस दिल पे बजुज़ दाग़े-नदामत[12]

फिर देखे हैं तो हिज्र के तपते हुए दिन भी
जब फ़िक्रे-दिलो-जां में फ़ुगां भूल गई है
हर शब वो सियह बोझ कि दिल बैठ गया है
हर सुब्ह की लौ तीर-सी सीने में लगी है

→

Khairiyat-e-jaan, raahate-tan, sehate-daaman
sub bhool gayeen maslahten ahle-havas ki

Is raah mein jo sab pe guzarti hai woh guzri
tanha pase-zindan, kabhi ruswa sarey-bazaar
Garje hain bahut sheikh sarey-gosha-e-mimbar
karke hain bahut ahle-hukam bar-sarey-darbaar

Chhora nahin gairon ne koi navke-dushnaam
chhuti nahin apno se koi tarze-malamat
Is ishq na us ishq pe naadim hai magar dil
har daag hai is dil pe bajuz dagey-nadamat
Phir dekhe hain to hizre ke tapte hue din bhi
jab phikre-dilo-jaan mein phogaan bhool gai hai
Har shab woh siyah bojh ki dil baith gaya hai
har subah ki lau teer-si seene mein lagi hai

All physical comfort, even safety of life, personal well-being
And all counsels of the wise world
I ignored.

And in this path, I suffered as everybody else does
Sometimes behind the bars alone, sometimes humiliation in public.
While the priests have thundered from the pulpit
And rulers have held out threats dire.

O In the foulest manner, have the adversaries abused
And most comprehensively have our own condemned
But I regret neither this love nor that all the same
And though every other scar my heart has
Not shame.

And then, I have seen those seering days of separation too
When smothered by anguish, I had forgotten even to sigh
When dark nights were a burden that crushed the heart
And daybreak was an arrow that pierced it through.

→

---

1. जान की खैरियत 2. तन का सुख 3. बिन फटा दामन 4. लोलुपों की 5. कारागार में 6. बीच बाज़ार में 7. उपदेश-मंच के कोने से 8. बादशाह 9. बीच दरबार में 10. गाली का तीर 11. भर्त्सना का ढंग 12. शरमिंदगी के दाग़ के सिवा

तन्हाई में क्या-क्या न तुझे याद किया है
        क्या-क्या न दिले-ज़ार ने ढूंढ़ी हैं पनाहें
आंखों से लगाया है कभी दस्ते-सबा को[1]
        डाली हैं कभी गर्दने-महताब में[2] बांहें

चाहा है इसी रंग में लैलाए-वतन को[3]
        तड़पा है इसी तौर से[4] दिल उसकी लगन में
ढूंढ़ी है युंही शौक़ ने[5] आसाइशे-मंज़िल[6]
        रुख़्सार के[7] ख़म में कभी काकुल की[8] शिकन[9] में

इस जाने-जहां को भी यूंही क़ल्बो-नज़र ने[10]
        हंस-हंस के सदा[11] दी, कभी रो-रो के पुकारा
पूरे किये सब हर्फ़े-तमन्ना के[12] तक़ाज़े
        हर दर्द को उजियाला, हर इक ग़म को संवारा

Tanhai mein kya-kya na tujhe yaad kiya hai
        kya-kya na dile-zaar ne dhundhi hain panahen
Aankhon se lagaya hai kabhi daste-saba ko
        daali hain kabhi gardane-mehtaab mein baanhen

Chaha hai isee rang mein lailaye-vatan ko
        tarpa hai isee taur se dil uski lagan mein
Dhundhi hain yunhi shauq ne aasaishe-manzil
        rukhsaar ke kham mein kabhi kaakul ki shikan mein

Is jaane-jahan ko bhi yunhi qalbo-nazar ne
        hans-hans ke sada di, kabhi ro-ro ke pukara
Purey kiye sab hurphe-tamanna ke taqaze
        har dard ko ujiyala, her ik ghum ko sanwara

---

1. प्रभात-समीर रूपी हाथ को 2. चांद की गर्दन में 3. देश-रूपी प्रेमिका 4. तरह से 5. इश्क़ ने 6. मंज़िल का सुख 7. कपोल के 8. केशों की 9. बल 10. दिल और नज़र ने 11. आवाज़ 12. अभिलाषा के

In hours of separation, how sorely I remembered you
How passionately has my heart your presence sought
How I have kissed the morning breeze with my eyes
sometimes
How often I hugged the moon to my heart!

So have I loved the other beloved, my country too
Similarly I have felt and pined for her
And like a pilgrim sought my heaven
In her beauty and charm;

So have my heart and sight called out to that
sweetheart
Sometimes smilingly, with tears sometime,
No demand of hers, I ignored, no summon
unanswered went
And all grief made light, all suffering endured.

फ़िक्रे-सूदो-जियां[1] तो छूटेगी
मिन्नते-ईनो-आं[2] तो छूटेगी
दोज़ख[3] में खैर मय[4] मिले न मिले
शेख साहब से जां तो छूटेगी

Phikre-sudo-jiyan to chhutegi
minnate-eeno-aan to chhutegi
dozakh mein khair mai miley na miley
sheikh sahab se jaan to chhutegi

1. लाभ-हानि की चिन्ता 2. ऐरा-ग़ैरा 3. नर्क 4. शराब

I will be free from worrying about gain and loss at least
And will not have to please all and sundry
I may or may not get wine in hell,
I will be at least rid of the Sheikhji

आये कुछ अब्र[1], कुछ शराब आये
इसके बाद आये जो अज़ाब[2] आये

हर रगे-जां में फिर चराग़ां[3] हो
सामने फिर वो बेनक़ाब आये

उम्र के हर वरक़[4] पे दिल को नज़र
तेरी मेहरो-वफ़ा के बाब[5] आये

कर रहा था ग़मे-जहाँ का हिसाब
आज तुम याद बेहिसाब आये

न गयी तेरे ग़म की सरदारी
दिल में यों रोज़ इन्कलाब आये

फैज़ थी राह सर-बसर मंज़िल
हम जहाँ पहुँचे कामयाब आये

Aaye kuchh abre, kuchh sharaab aaye
iske baad aaye jo azaab aaye

Her rage-jaan mein phir charage ho
saamne phir woh benaqab aaye

Umre ke her varak pe dil ko nazar
teri mehro-wafa ke baab aaye

Kar raha tha game-jahan ka hisaab
aaj tum yaad behisaab aaye

Na gayi tere gham ki sardari
dil mein yon roz inqilaab aaye

Faiz thi raah sar-basar manzil
hum jahan pahunche kamyaab aaye

---

1. बादल 2. मुसीबत 3. दीपावली 4. पन्ना 5. अध्याय

Let there be some clouds, some wine
And then any retribution is fine

Let there be light in every blood-vein
Let her come before me unveiled again

On every page of the life's book, the heart could see
Chapters of your kindness, cantos of your loyalty

Going over the sorrows of life today
I remembered you all the way

It could never break away from your love's sway
Although revolt has been my heart's way

I met my destination wherever I went
My life's journey, O Faiz, was fully triumphant

तन्हाई

फिर कोई आया दिले-ज़ार[1]! नहीं, कोई नहीं
राहरौ[2] होगा, कहीं और चला जाएगा

ढल चुकी रात बिखरने लगा तारों का गुबार
लड़खड़ाने लगे एवानों में[3] ख़्वाबीदा[4] चिराग़
सो गई रास्ता तक-तक के हर इक राहग़ुज़र[5]
अजनबी ख़ाक ने धुंधला दिए क़दमों के सुराग़[6]
गुल करो[7] शम्ए, बढ़ा दो मय-ओ-मीना-ओ-अयाग़[8]

अपने बेख़्वाब[9] किवाड़ों को मुक़फ़्फल कर लो[10]
अब यहां कोई नहीं, कोई नहीं आएगा

Phir koi aaya diley-zaar! nahin, koi nahin
raahrau hoga, kahin aur chala jayega

Dhal chuki raat bikharne laga taron ka gubaar
larkharane lagey aiwano mein khwabida chiraag
so gai raasta tak-tak ke her ik raahguzar
ajnabi khaaq ne dhundhla diye kadmon ke suraag
gul karo shamae, badha do mai-o-meena-o-ayaag

Apne bekhwab kiwaron ko muqaffal kar lo
ab yahan koi nahin, koi nahin aayega

---

1. दुखी मन 2. राही 3. महलों में 4. सोये हुए 5. मार्ग 6. चिह्न 7. बुझा दो 8. सुराही, प्याले और शराब उठा दो 9. जिनकी आंखों में नींद नहीं 10. ताले लगा लो

Loneliness 

Has somebody come, O sad heart? No, none at all,
It must be some passer-by, who will go his way;

The night is ending and the stars are dispersing,
apart,
The sleepy candles in the palaces sputter
And every pathway after a long wait has fallen asleep
The uncaring dust has obiliterated all foot-marks—
Blow out the candle, and remove the bottle and the
chalice hence,

Close your sleepless eyes like a house locked
Nobody, nobody will come here now.

शायर लोग

हरेक दौर में हम, हर ज़माने में हम
ज़हर पीते रहे, गीत गाते रहे
जान देते रहे ज़िन्दगी के लिए
साअत-ए-वस्ल[1] की सरखुशी[2] के लिए
दीन-ओ-दुनिया की दौलत लुटाते रहे
फक्र-ओ-फ़ाका[3] का तोशा[4] सँभाले हुए
जो भी रस्ता चुना उस पे चलते रहे
माल वाले हिकारत[5] से तकते रहे
तान[6] करते रहे, हाथ मलते रहे

हमने उन पर किया हर्फ़-ए-हक[7] संग-ज़न[8]
जिन की हैबत[9] से दुनिया लरज़ती रही
जिन पे आँसू बहाने को कोई न था
अपनी आँख उनके ग़म में बरसती रही
सबसे ओझल हुए हुक्म-ए-हाकिम पे हम
क़ैदख़ाने सहे, ताज़याने[10] सहे।

लोग सुनते रहे साज़-ए-दिल की सदा
अपने नग़मे सलाख़ों से छनते रहे

→

Harek daur mein hum, har zamane mein hum
zahar pitey rahe, geet gaate rahe
jaan dete rahe zindagi ke liye
saaet-e-vasl ki sarkhushi ke liye
deen-o-duniya ki daulat lutate rahe
fakra-o-faqa ka tosha sambhale hue
jo bhi rasta chuna us pe chalte rahe
maal wale hikarat se takte rahe
taan karte rahe haath malte rahe

Humne un par kiya hurf-e-huq sang-zan
jinki haibat se duniya larazti rahi
jin pe aansu bahane ko koi na tha
apni aankh unke ghum mein barasti rahi
sabse ojhal hue huqm-e-hakim pe hum
qaidkhane sahe taazyane sahe
log sunte rahe saaz-e-dil ki sada
apne naghme salakhon se chhante rahe

The Poets

In every era, in every age
We drank poison, we sang songs
And died so that life survives
And hours of union live.
We have lived in poverty and hunger
Sacrificed whatever we have had
But always our chosen path pursued.
Looked down upon by the rich,
Taunted and resented

We have thrown back on them
Stories of truth.
For the lonely and the terrorized our hearts have wept.
The powers that be banished us
Whipped us, threw us in jail

And from behind the bars our songs have wafted out.

→

1. मिलन की घड़ी 2. मस्ती की चरम सीमा 3. निर्धनता और भूख 4. सामग्री 5. घृणा 6. व्यंग्य 7. सत्य-वचन 8. पत्थर मारने वाला 9. भयभीत होना 10. कोड़े

खूँचकाँ[1] दह्र[2] का खूँचकाँ आईना
दुख भरे ख़ल्क़[3] का दुख भरा दिल हैं हम
तब्अ-ए-शाएर[4] हैं जंगाह-ए-अद्ल-ओ-सितम[5]
मुन्सिफ-ए-खैर-ओ-शर[6] हक़्क़-ओ-बातिल[7] हैं हम

सहल यूँ राह-ए-ज़िन्दगी की है
हर क़दम हमने आशिक़ी की है
हमने दिल में सजा लिये गुलशन
जब बहारों ने बेरुख़ी की है
ज़हर से धो लिये हैं होंठ अपने
लुत्फ़-ए-साक़ी [8] ने जब कमी की है
तेरे कूचे में बादशाही की
जब से निकले गदागरी [9] की है
बस वही सुर्खरू हुआ जिसने
बहर-ए-खूँ में शनावरी[10] की है
"जो गुज़रते थे दाग़ पर सदमे"
अब वही कैफ़ियत सभी की है (लन्दन, 1979)

Khunchkaan dehar ka khunchkaan aaina
dukh bhare khalk ka dukh bhara dil hain hum
tabae-e-shayar hain jangaah-e-adal-o-sitam
munsif-e-khair-o-shar haqk-o-baatil hain hum

Sehal yun raah-e-zindagi ki hai
har kadam humne aashiqi ki hai
humne dil mein saja liye gulshan
jab baharon ne berukhi ki hai
zahar se dho liye hain honth apne
lutf-e-saaqi ne jab kami ki hai
tere kuche mein baadshahi ki
jab se nikle gadagari ki hai
bus wahi surkhru hua jisne
behar-e-khoon mein shanawari ki hai
'jo guzarte the daag par sadme'
ab wahi kaifiyat sabhi ki hai

A blood-soaked mirror of the blood-soaked world
We are the sad soul of suffering humanity;
We are the poets, we are the conscience-keeper, we are the Judges
In this battle between tyranny and justice, good and evil, falsehood and truth.

Whenever the spring season turned its back on us
In our heart, we have felt the flowers blooming,
We have loved everybody around
And thus made our life liveable,
Soaking our lips with poison.
Whenever the Saqi turned niggardly.
Only those who have swum through a sea of blood,
Only they have gone across—
In suffering, we are in the same boat
As 'Daagh' was, when he spoke of his sorrows.

---

1. खून टपकाना 2. ज़माना 3. जनता 4. अन्तरात्मा के कवि 5. जुल्म और इन्साफ़ की रणभूमि 6. अच्छाई और बुराई के बीच इन्साफ़ करने वाला 7. सत्य और असत्य 8. साक़ी की मेहरबानी 9. भीख माँगना 10. तैरना

रहे-ख़िज़ां में[1] तलाशे-बहार करते रहे
शबे-सियह से[2] तलबे-हुस्ने-यार करते रहे[3]

ख़याले-यार कभी, ज़िक्रे-यार करते रहे
इसी मताअ पे[4] हम रोज़गार करते रहे

नहीं शिकायते-हिज्रां[5] कि इस वसीले से[6]
हम उनसे रिश्ता-ए-दिल उस्तवार[7] करते रहे

वो दिन कि कोई भी जब वजहे-इन्तिज़ार न थी
हम उनमें तेरा सवा[8] इन्तिज़ार करते रहे

उन्हीं के फ़ैज़[9] से बाज़ारे-अक्ल[10] रौशन है
जो गाह-गाह[11] जुनूं[12] इख़्तियार करते रहे

Rahe-khizaan mein talashe-bahaar karte rahe
shabe-siyah se talbe-husne-yaar karte rahe

Khayale-yaar kabhi, zikre-yaar karte rahe
isee matae pe hum rozgaar karte rahe

Nahin shikayate-hizran ki is vasile se
hum unse rishta-e-dil ustvaar karte rahe

Woh din ki koi bhi jab vazhe-intizaar na thi
hum unmein tera sava intizaar karte rahe

Unhin ke Faiz se bazare-akal raushan hai
jo gaah-gaah junoon ikhtiyaar karte rahe

---

1. पतझड़ के मार्ग में 2. काली, अंधियारी रात से 3. यार या प्रेमिका का सौन्दर्य मांगते रहे 4. पूंजी पर 5. वियोग की शिकायत 6. साधन से 7. दृढ़ 8. और अधिक 9. कृपा 10. बुद्धिरूपी बाज़ार 11. कभी-कभी 12. उन्माद

I look for spring in the autumn season
And in the thick dark night, seek my beauteous one

Sometime, I think of my love, some time, I speak of her
This is the vocation that provides me succour

I seek to relate to her through my heart
So I never complain when from her I part

I await all the more keenly, your coming
On days when there is no reason whatever for waiting

Only because of them, O Faiz, for whom occasionally passion is everything.
Only because of them, reason is the king.

ढलती है मौजे-मय[1] की तरह रात इन दिनों
खिलती है सुबह गुल की तरह रंगों-बू से पुर
वीरां है जाम पास करो कुछ बहार का
दिल आरज़ू से पुर करो, आँखें लहू से पुर

Dhalti hai mauje-mai ki tarah raat in dino
khiltee hai subah gul ki tarah rangon-bu se pur
viraan hai jaam paas karo kuchh bahaar ka
dil aarzu se pur karo, aankhen lahoo se pur

1. शराब की धार

The night comes these days like the wine, flowing
The dawn resembles a colourful fragrant flower
The cup is empty, at least for the sake of spring season
Fill your eyes with blood, your heart with desire

निसार मैं तेरी गलियों पे

निसार मैं तेरी गलियों पे ऐ वतन, कि जहां
चली है रस्म कि कोई न सर उठा के चले
जो कोई चाहने वाला तवाफ़ को[1] निकले
नज़र चुरा के चले, जिस्मो-जां बचा के चले
है अहले-दिल के लिए अब ये नज़्मे-बस्तो-कुशाद[2]
कि संगो-ख़िश्त[3] मुक़य्यद[4] हैं और सग[5] आज़ाद
बहुत हैं ज़ुल्म के दस्ते-बहाना-जू[6] के लिए
जो चन्द अहले-जुनूं तेरे नाम-लेवा हैं
बने हैं अहले-हवस[7] मुद्दई भी, मुन्सिफ़ भी
किसे वकील करें, किससे मुन्सिफ़ी चाहें
मगर गुज़ारने वालों के दिन गुज़रते हैं
तेरे फ़िराक़ में यूं सुब्हो-शाम करते हैं
बुझा जो रौज़ने-ज़िंदां[8] तो दिल ये समझा है
कि तेरी मांग सितारों से भर गई होगी
चमक उठे हैं सलासिल[9] तो हमने जाना है
कि अब सहर[10] तेरे रुख़ पर[11] बिखर गई होगी

→

Nisaar main teri galiyon pe ae vatan, ki jahan
chali hai rasm ki koi na sar utha ke chale
jo koi chahne wala tawaaf ko nikle
nazar chura ke chale, jismo-jaan bacha ke chale
Hai ahle-dil ke liye ab ye nazme-basto-kushaad
ki sango-khisht muqayyad hain aur sag azaad
Bahut hain zulm ke daste-bahana-joo ke liye
jo chand ahle-junoon tere naam-lewa hain
bane hain ahle-havas muddai bhi, munsif bhi
kise vakeel karen, kis se munsifi chahen
Magar guzarne walon ke din guzarte hain
tere firaq mein yun subho-shaam karte hain
Bujha jo rauzane-zindan to dil ye samjha hai
ki teri maang sitaron se bhar gai hogi
chamak uthe hain salasil to humne jaana hai
ki ab sehar tere rukh per bikhar gai hogi

Let me bow before You ❀

Let me bow before you, my country, where
It is ordained that none will walk the streets with
his head held high
And if some lover of yours must go around
He should go most cautiously with downcast eyes,
Where under the new rules of freedom and
discipline,
Dogs are at large while brick and stones are held
in thrall.

However, there are still enough of your lovers around
To take on the tyrant there,
Though there is many a greedy one too
Who has become both a prosecutor and a Judge;
And we know not whom to make our lawyer
And from where can we justice get—
Still we live on
And pass our days and nights remembering you.

Whenever through the prison window we look
outside in the dark
We surmise that the parting in your hair is filled with
stars
Whenever our fetters shine in the light, we imagine
That your face is glowing in the morning sun—

→

1. परिक्रमा के लिए 2. बंधन और मुक्ति की व्यवस्था 3. ईंट-पत्थर 4. क़ैद 5. कुत्ते 6. बहाना बनाने वाले के हाथ 7. लोलुप 8. कारागार का झरोखा 9. बेड़ियां 10. सुबह 11. मुखड़े पर

ग़रज़ तसव्वुरे-शामो-सहर में[1] जीते हैं
गिरफ्ते-साया-ए-दीवारो-दर में[2] जीते हैं
युंही हमेशा उलझती रही है ज़ुल्म से ख़ल्क़[3]
न उनकी रस्म नई है, न अपनी रीत नई
युंही हमेशा खिलाए हैं हमने आग में फूल
न उनकी हार नई है न अपनी जीत नई
इसी सबब से फ़लक का गिला नहीं करते
तेरे फ़िराक़ में हम दिल बुरा नहीं करते
गर आज तुझसे जुदा हैं तो कल बहम[4] होंगे
ये रात भर की जुदाई तो कोई बात नहीं
गर आज औज पे[5] है तालए-रक़ीब[6] तो क्या
ये चार दिन की खुदाई तो कोई बात नहीं
जो तुझसे अहदो-वफ़ा उस्तुवार[7] रखते हैं
इलाजे-गर्दिशे लैलो-निहार[8] रखते हैं

(जेल में लिखी नज़्म)

Garaz tasavure-shamo-sehar mein jitey hain
girafte-saya-e-deewaro-dar mein jitey hain
Yunhi hamesha ulajhti rahi hai zulm se khalq
na unki rasm nai hai, ne apni reet nai
yunhi hamesha khilaye hain humne aag mein phool
na unki haar nai hai na apni jeet nai
Isee sabab se falak ka gila nahin karte
tere firaq mein hum dil bura nahin karte
Gar aaj tujhse juda hain to kal beham honge
ye raat bhar ki judaai to koi baat nahin
gar aaj auj pe hai taalae-raqib to kya
ye char din ki khudaai to koi baat nahin
Jo tujhse ahdo-wafa ustuwaar rakhte hain
ilaaje-gardishe lailo-nihar rakhte hain

---

1. सुबह और शाम की कल्पना में 2. दीवारों और दरवाज़ों के सायों की पकड़ में 3. जनता 4. इकट्ठे 5. आकाश पर 6. प्रतिद्वन्द्वी का भाग्य 7. प्रेम निभाने की प्रतिज्ञा को सुदृढ़ 8. रात-दिन के क्रम का इलाज

That is, behind bars, though,
We live lost in thoughts of you.

Like this only, have the people fought tyranny
There is nothing new about it all—
Always like this, we have grown flowers in the fire
There is nothing new in their defeat and nothing new about our victory, so
We don't mind our fate
Or feel sad that we are away from you
For, if we are separated today, we'll certainly meet tomorrow.
This separation of a mere night is a separation hardly
And if the enemy's star is on the ascendant today
It matters not,
For this temporary divinity is no divinity at all—

And those who are committed to love you
Know also how to tide over this lean phase too.

आज बाज़ार में पाबजौला चलो

आज बाज़ार में पाबजौला[1] चलो
चश्मे-नम, जाने-शोरीदा[2] काफ़ी नहीं
तोहमे इश्क़ पोशीदा[3] काफ़ी नहीं
आज बाज़ार में पाबजौला चलो

दस्ते अफ़शां[4] चलो, मस्तो रक्सां[5] चलो
खाक बरसर[6] चलो खूबदामां[7] चलो
राह तकता है सब शहरे-जानां चलो

हाकमे-शहर भी, मुहबे-आम[8] भी
तीरे-इलज़ाम भी, संगे-दुश्नाम[9] भी
सुबहे-नाशाद,[10] भी रोज़े-नाकाम भी
इनका दमसाज़ अपने सिवा कौन है
शहरे-जानां में अब वासफा[11] कौन है
दस्ते-कातिल के शायां[12] रहा कौन है
रुख्सते-दिल बांध लो, दिलफिगारो चलो
फिर हमीं कत्ल हो आयें यारो चलो।

Aaj bazaar mein pa bajaulan chalo
chashme-num jaane-shorida kaafi nahin
tohame ishq poshida kaafi nahin
aaj bazaar mein pa bajaulan chalo

Daste-afshan chalo, masto raksan chalo
khaq varsar chalo khoobdaman chalo
raah takta hai sab shehrey-jaana chalo

Haaqme-shehar bhi, muhbe-aam bhi
tiray-ilzaam bhi, sangey-darnam bhi
subhey-nashad bhi, roze-nakaam bhi
inka damsaaz apne siwa kaun hai
shehray-jaana mein ab vasafa kaun hai
daste-qaatil ke shaayan raha kaun hai
rukhsate-dil baandh lo, dilfigaro chalo
phir hamin qatl ho aayen yaaro chalo

---

1. बेड़ियों में 2. दुःखी आत्मा 3. छिपी हुई 4. हाथ घुमाते हुए 5. नाचते हुए 6. सर पर खाक डाले हुए 7. खून से लथपथ 8. आम लोग 9. बदनामी का पत्थर 10. दुखी 11. लामबंद 12 योग्य

Go to the Market Place in Fetters Today 

Moist eyes are not enough, nor the tortured soul
Nor would the allegation of concealed love do,
Go to the marketplace in fetters

Besmear your head with dust, daub your dress with blood
Shuffle your hands around, twist and turn.
Come on, the city of your beloved is looking on,

The commoners are gathered, the rulers are there.
The arrows of allegation, the missiles of infamy
The morning sorrowful, the days of failure—
Who else could bear all of these,
Who else is pure enough in the city of the beloved,
Except us
To win the assassin's hand?
Take your sorrowing heart with you, let's go
Once again

O comrades, let's go and be slain.

आज़ादी की सुबह : अगस्त 1947

ये दाग़-दाग़ उजाला, ये शब-गुज़ीद[1] सहर
वो इन्तज़ार था जिसका ये वो सहर तो नहीं
ये वो सहर तो नहीं जिसकी आरज़ू लेकर
चले थे यार कि मिल जायेगी कहीं न कहीं
फ़लक[2] के दश्त[3] पे तारों की आखरी मंज़िल
कहीं तो शबे-सुस्ते-मौज का साहिल
कहीं तो जाके उतरेगा सफीना[4]-ए-ग़मे दिल
जवां लहू की पुरइसरार शाहराहों में
चले जो यार तो दामन पे कितने हाथ पड़े

दयारे-हुस्न[5] की बेसब्र ख्वाबगाहों[6] से
पुकारती रहीं बांहें, बदन बुलाते रहे
बहुत अजीज़ थी लेकिन रुखे-सहर[7] की लगन
बहुत करीं[8] था हसीनाने-नूर[9] का दामन
सबुक-सबुक थी तमन्ना, दबी-दबी थी थकन →

Ye daag-daag ujala, ye shab-guzeed sehar
wo intizaar tha jiska ye woh sehar to nahin
ye woh sehar to nahin jiski aarzu lekar
chale the yaar ki mil jayegi kahin na kahin
falak ke dasht pe taron ki aakhri manzil
kahin to shabe-suste-mauj ka sahil
kahin to jaake utrega safina-e-ghame dil
jawan lahoo ki purisraar shahrahon mein
chale jo yaar to daaman pe kitney haath pare

Dayarey-husn ki besabra khawabgahon se
pukarti rahi baanhen, badan bulate rahe
bahut ajeez thi lekin rukhe-sehar ki lagan
bahut karin tha hasinane-noor ka daaman
sabuk-sabuk thi tamanna, dabi-dabi thi thakan

---

1. रात की डसी हुई 2. आसमान 3. जंगल 4. किश्ती 5. हुस्न का शहर 6. शयनगृह 7. सुबह का चेहरा 8. नज़दीक 9. रोशनी

The Dawn of Freedom—August 1947

This light all stained, the morning bitten by night
This is not the dawn we looked forward to,
This is not the dawn we set out for,
Hoping that somewhere in the wildness of the sky
There must be the final destination of stars,
Somewhere the slow languorous night
Will meet its shore
And somewhere ultimately the heart's agony will end.

Youthful and determined, as we comrades set out
Countless hands caught us by the sleeve
Seductive arms and bodies
Kept beckoning us from their dreamy bed chambers,
But we held the face of the dawn so dear
And the hem of luminous beauty looked so near,
While we experienced mild fatigue and delicate
longing.

→

सुना है हो भी चुका है फ़िराक़े-ज़ुल्मतो-नूर[1]
सुना है हो भी चुका है विसाले-मंज़िलो-गाम[2]
बदल चुका है बहुत कुछ अहले-दर्द का दस्तूर
निशातो-वस्ल[3] *हलाल, अज़ाबो-हिज्र*[4] *हराम*

जिगर की आग, नज़र की उमंग, दिल की जलन
किसी पे चारा-ए-हिज्रां[5] *का कुछ असर ही नहीं*
कहाँ से आई निगारे-सुबह, किधर गयी
अभी चराग़े-सरे-रह[6] *को कुछ पता ही नहीं*

अभी गरानी-ए-शब[7] *में कमी नहीं आई*
निजाते-दीदा-ओ-दिल[8] *की घड़ी नहीं आयी*
चले चलो कि वो मंज़िल अभी नहीं आयी

Suna hai ho bhi chuka hai firaqey-zulmato-noor
suna hai ho bhi chuka hai visale-manzilo-gaam
badal chuka hai bahut kuchh ahle-dard ka dastoor
nishato-vasl halaal, azabo-hizra haraam

Jigar ki aag, nazar ki umang, dil ki jalan
kisi pe chara-e-hizran ka kuchh asar hi nahin
kahan se aai-nigarey-subah, kidhar gai
abhi charagey-sarey-reh ko kuchh pata hi nahin

Abhi garani-e-shab mein kami nahin aai
nijatey-deeda-o-dil ki ghari nahin aai
chale chalo ki woh manzil abhi nahin aai

---

1. अंधेरे और रोशनी का अलगाव 2. मंज़िल आ भी चुकी है 3. मिलन का सुख 4. जुदाई का डर 5. जुदाई का इलाज 6. सुबह का चराग़ 7. रात का भारीपन 8. दिल और आँख की खुशी

Now, we hear that light and darkness have already parted
The quest has already its destination met
And the age of agony already ended
Joys of union granted, pains of separation banished.

The burning in the bosom, however
The fire in the heart and desire in the eye—
The anguish of separation is intact yet;
From where the morning breeze came, which way it went,
The street lamp has no knowledge at all.

The heaviness of night is still as it was.
The hour of deliverance for the heart and eye
Has not yet arrived
Press on, for the destination is yet to be reached.

न आज लुत्फ़ कर इतना कि, कल गुज़र न सके
वो रात जो तेरे गेसुओं की रात नहीं
ये आरज़ू भी बड़ी चीज़ है मगर हमदम
विसाले-यार[1] फ़कत[2] आरज़ू की बात नहीं

Na aaj lutf kar itna ki, kal guzar na sake
woh raat jo tere gesuon ki raat nahin
ye aarzoo bhi bari cheej hai magar humdum
visaley-yaar fakat aarzoo ki baat nahin

1. मित्र से मिलना 2. केवल

Don't give me so much happiness today
That tomorrow, I cannot pass the night bereft of you,
Desire is certainly important, but O friend,
For meeting the beloved, desire alone would not do.

दोनों जहान तेरी मोहब्बत में हार के
वो जा रहा है कोई शबे-ग़म गुज़ार के

वीरां है मैकदा ख़ुमो-साग़र[1] उदास हैं
तुम क्या गए कि रूठ गए दिन बहार के

इक फ़ुर्सते-गुनाह[2] मिली, वो भी चार दिन
देखे हैं हमने हौसले परवरदिगार के[3]

दुनिया ने तेरी याद से बेगाना कर दिया
तुझ से भी दिलफ़रेब[4] हैं ग़म रोज़गार के

भूले से मुस्करा तो दिए थे वो आज 'फ़ैज़'
मत पूछ वलवले दिले-नाकर्दाकार के[5]

Dono jahan teri mohabbat mein haar ke
woh ja raha hai koi shabe-ghum guzaar ke

Viraan hai maiqada khumo-sagar udaas hain
tum kya gaye ki rooth gaye din bahaar ke

Ik phursate-gunaah milee, woh bhi char din
dekhe hain humne hausale parvardigar ke

Duniya ne teri yaad se begana kar diya
tujh se bhi dilfareb hain ghum rozgaar ke

Bhule se muskara to diye the who aaj 'Faiz'
mat puchh walvale diley-nakardakaar ke

---

1. शराब का प्याला और मटकी 2. पाप करने का अवकाश 3. भगवान के 4. हृदयाकर्षक 5. अनुभवहीन दिल के

In your love, having both the worlds lost
There goes one, his night of suffering past

Deserted is the tavern, the jar and cup are desolate too
You have taken away the spring season also alongwith you

Only a few days I got even to sin
Too well have I seen the generosity of heaven

The world has overshadowed your remembrance too
The cares of life are closer to the heart than even you

Quite unwitting today, she smiled, O Faiz
And what a flood of longings my poor heart has !

मेरे नदीम

ख़यालो-शे'र[1] की दुनिया में जान थी जिनसे
फ़िज़ाए-फ़िक्रो-अमल[2] अरग़वान[3] थी जिनसे
वो जिनके नूर[4] से शादाब[5] थे महो-अंजुम[6]
जुनूने-इश्क़ की हिम्मत जवान थी जिनसे
वो आर्ज़ूएं[7] कहां सो गई हैं मेरे नदीम!
वो नासबूर[8] निगाहें, वो मुन्तज़िर राहें
वो पासे-ज़ब्त[9] से दिल में दबी हुई आहें
वो इन्तिज़ार की रातें, तवील[10], तीरा-व-तीर[11]
वो नीम-ख़्वाब शबिस्तां[12], वो मख़मली बांहें
कहानियां थीं, कहीं खो गई हैं मेरे नदीम!
मचल रहा है रगे-ज़िन्दगी में ख़ूने-बहार
उलझ रहे हैं पुराने ग़मों से रूह के तार
चलो, कि चलके चिराग़ां[13] करें दियारे-हबीब[14]
हैं इन्तिज़ार में अगली[15] मोहब्बतों के मज़ार[16]
मोहब्बतें जो फ़ना[17] हो गई हैं मेरे नदीम!

Khayalo-sher ki duniya mein jaan thi jinse
phizaye-phikro-amal argawan thi jinse
woh jinke noor se shadaab the maho-anjum
junoone-ishq ki himmat jawan thi jinse
Woh aarzuen kahan so gai hain mere nadeem !
Woh nasaboor nigahen woh muntazir raahein
woh paase-zabat se dil mein dabi hui aahen
woh intizaar ki raaten, taveel, tira-v-teer
woh neem-khawb shabista, woh makhmali baanhen
Kahaniyan thin, kahin kho gai hain mere nadeem !
Machal raha hai rage-zindagi mein khoone-bahaar
ulajh rahe hain purane-ghamon se rooh ke taar
chalo, ki chalke chiraagan karen diyare-habeeb
hain intizaar mein agali mohabbaton ke mazaar
Mohabbaten jo fana ho gai hain mere nadeem !

---

1. विचार और काव्य 2. विचार और कर्म का वातावरण 3. लाल (रंगीन) 4. ज्योति 5. आप्लावित, परिपूर्ण 6. चांद-तारे 7. आकांक्षाएं 8. बेचैन, अधीर 9. सहन करने की लिहाज़ 10. लम्बी 11. अन्धकारपूर्ण 12. अर्ध-निद्रित शयनागार 13. दीपमाला 14. प्रिय मित्र का घर 15. पुरानी 16. प्रेम की समाधियां 17. विनष्ट

My Friend

The aspirations, that spurred our thought, inspired
our verse
And gave a glow to all our deeds,
The aspirations, that lent luster to the moon and the
stars,
Gave strength and perseverance to our love
Where have they gone, my friend!

Those insatiable eyes, those pathways waiting for us
Those sighs by social etiquettes kept in check,
Those nights of waiting, dark and long,
Those bedroom half-awake, those satin arms
Which feel like fairy tales now,
Where have they been lost, my friend!

Life is bubbling with fresh blood
And old wounds are coming alive—
Let's go and illuminate our beloved's house,
Illuminate the sepulchers of past love,
Loves which are perished and are seen no more,
my friend!

शाम

इस तरह है कि हर इक पेड़ कोई मन्दिर है
कोई उजड़ा हुआ बेनूर[1] पुराना मन्दिर
ढूंढ़ता है जो ख़राबी के बहाने कब से!
चाक हर बाम[2], हर इक दर का दमे-आख़िर[3] है
आस्मां कोई पुरोहित है जो हर बाम तले
जिस्म पर राख मले, माथे पे सेंदूर मले
सर-नगूं[4] बैठा है चुप-चाप न जाने कब से!
इस तरह है कि पसे-पर्दा[5] कोई साहिर[6] है
जिसने आफ़ाक़ पे[7] डाला किसी सिह्र[8] का दाम
दामने-वक़्त से[9] पैवस्त[10] है यूं दामने-शाम!
अब कभी शाम बुझेगी न अंधेरा होगा
अब कभी रात ढलेगी न सवेरा होगा
आस्मां आस लिए है कि ये जादू टूटे
चुप की ज़ंजीर कटे, वक़्त का दामन टूटे
दे कोई संख दुहाई, कोई पायल बोले
कोई बुत जागे, कोई सांवली घूंघट खोले!

Is tarah hai ki har ik peir koi mandir hai
koi ujra hua benoor purana mandir
Dhundhta hai jo kharabi ke bahane kab se !
Chaak har baam, har ik dar ka dame-aakhir hai
aasmaan koi purohit hai jo har baam tale
jism par raakh maley, maathe pe sindoor maley
Sar-nagoon baitha hai chup-chaap na jaane kab se !
Is tarah hai ki pase-parda koi sahir hai
jisne aaphaaq pe daala kisi sinh ka daam
Daamne-waqt se paivast hai yoon daamne-shaam !
Ab kabhi shaam bujhegi na andhera hoga
ab kabhi raat dhalegi na savera hoga
aasmaan aas liye hai ki ye jadu tutey
chup ki zanjeer katey, waqt ka daman tutey
de koi sankh duhai, koi payal boley
Koi but jagey, koi sanwali ghunghat kholey

---

1. प्रकाशहीन 2. टूटी हुई छत 3. अन्तिम समय 4. सिर झुकाए 5. पर्दे के पीछे 6. जादूगर 7. आकाश पर 8. जादू 9. समय रूपी दामन से 10. जुड़ा हुआ

The Evening

It appears that every tree is a shrine,
An old shrine, dark and desolate, with every door and window cracking;
The sky is like a priest with his body
Besmeared with ash, and forehead, with vermillion, red
Sitting silent for ages with downcast head;

It appears that behind the curtain, there sits a magician
Who has cast his magic spell on the horizon
And the evening so envelops the atmosphere
As if it will never yield place to the dark night,
Which in turn will never allow the day to dawn;

The heavens are fervently hoping that the spell breaks,
This deathly silence ends and the times freely move apace,
Desperately waiting for some conch to blow, some anklet to speak,

Some idol to wake up and some veiled beauty to show its face.

हम से जितने सुखन तुम्हारे थे
हमने सब शे'र में संवारे थे

रंगो-खुशबू के, हुस्ने-खूबी के
तुम से थे जितने इश्तियारे[1] थे

तेरे कौलो-क़रार से पहले
अपने कुछ और भी सहारे थे

मेरे दामन में आकर गिरे सारे
जितने दश्ते-फ़लक[2] में तारे थे

उम्रे-जावेद की[3] दुआ करते
फैज़ इतने वो कब हमारे थे

Hum se jitne sukhan tumhare the
humne sab sher mein sanware the

Rango-khushboo ke, husne-khubi ke
tum se the jitne ishtiyare the

Tere kaulo-quarar se pehle
apne kuch aur bhi sahare the

Mere daaman mein aakar girey saare
jitne dashte-phalak mein taare the

Umre-javed ki dua karte
Faiz itne woh kab humare the

---

1. रूपक 2. आसमान रूपी जंगल 3. चिरजीवी होने की

Whatever you said to us
We used it all to adorn our verse

Metaphors of colour, fragrance and beauty
Emanated, all of them, from you only

Before the pledge made by you
I had other supports too

All the stars in heaven's platter
Fell in my lap, as they fell from there

O Faiz, she was never mine so much
That she would pray for my long life as such

आज की रात

आज की रात साज़े-दर्द न छेड़!
दुख से भरपूर दिन तमाम हुए
और कल की ख़बर किसे मालूम
दोशो-फ़र्दा की[1] मिट चुकी हैं हुदूद[2]
हो न हो अब सहर किसे मालूम
ज़िन्दगी हेच! लेकिन आज की रात
एज़दियत[3] है मुमकिन आज की रात
आज की रात साज़े-दर्द न छेड़!
अब न दोहरा, फ़साना-हाए-अलम[4]
अपनी क़िस्मत पे सोगवार[5] न हो
फ़िक्रे-फ़र्दा[6] उतार दे दिल से
उम्रे-रफ़्ता पे[7] अश्कबार न हो[8]
अहदे-ग़म की हिकायतें[9] मत पूछ
हो चुकीं सब शिकायतें, मत पूछ
आज की रात साज़े-दर्द न छेड़!

Aaj ki raat saaze-dard na chher !
Dukh se bharpoor din tamaam hue
aur kal ki khabar kise maloom
dosho-pharda ki mit chuki hain hudood
ho na ho ab sehar kise maloom
Zindagi hech! lekin aaj ki raat
aezdiyat hai mumkin aaj ki raat
aaj ki raat saaze dard ne chher!
Ab na dohra, fasana-hae-alam
apni kismat pe sogawar na ho
phikre-pharda utaar de dil se
umre-rafta pe ashqbaar na ho
Ahde-ghum ki hikayaten mat poochh
ho chukin sab shikayten, mat poochh
aaj ki raat saaze-dard na chher !

---

1. अतीत और भविष्य की 2. सीमाएं 3. खुदाई 4. दुःख की कहानियां 5. उदास 6. कल की चिन्ता 7. बीती आयु पर 8. आंसू न बहा 9. दुःख के दिनों की कहानियां

Tonight

Do not touch the chord of sorrow tonight.
The sufferings of today have come to an end
And about tomorrow, nobody knows;
The past and present merge tonight
Life is meaningless and there is no guarantee
though
Of the next day dawning,
We can act like gods tonight.
Tonight, touch not the chord of sorrow,
No use retelling the tale of woe,
Lament not your fate,
Free yourself of all care for the future
And shed no tears over the life gone by.
Less said the better, about sorrows past,
0 mention not your regrets, tonight
Tonight, touch not the chord of sorrow, pray.

खुदा वो वक्त न लाये

खुदा वो वक़्त न लाए कि सोगवार[1] हो तू !
सुकूं की[2] नींद तुझे भी हराम हो जाए
तेरी मसर्रते-पैहम[3] तमाम हो जाए
तेरी हयात[4] तुझे तल्ख़-जाम[5] हो जाए
ग़मों से आईना-ए-दिल[6] गुदाज़[7] हो तेरा !

हुजूमे-यास से[8] बेताब होके रह जाए
बफ़ूरे-दर्द से[9] सीमाब[10] होके रह जाए
तेरा शबाब[11] फ़क़त[12] ख़्वाब होके रह जाए
ग़रूरे-हुस्न[13] सरापा नियाज़[14] हो तेरा !

→

Khuda woh waqt na laaye ki sogawar ho tu !
Sukun ki nind tujhe bhi haraam ho jaaye
teri masarrate-pehum tamaam ho jaaye
teri hayat tujhe tulkh-jaam ho jaaye
ghamon se aaina-e-dil gudaaz ho tera !

Hujume-yaas se betaab hoke reh jaaye
bafure-dard se simaab hoke reh jaaye
tera shabaab phakat khwab hoke reh jaaye
garurey-husan sarapa niyaaz ho tera !

---

1. उदास, मलिन-मन 2. शान्ति की 3. स्थायी प्रसन्नता 4. जीवन 5. कड़वा प्याला 6. हृदय-रूपी दर्पण 7. द्रवण 8. निराशाओं के समूह से 9. पीड़ा की बहुलता से 10. पारा 11. यौवन 12. केवल 13. सौन्दर्य का घमंड 14. सिर से पैर तक विनय की मूर्ति

May God the Day Never Comes 

May God, the day never comes when you're sad,
When you too are unable to sleep a peaceful sleep,
When your days of delight are shattered,
Your life becomes a bed of thorns
And grief breaks your heart,

When your youth into a nightmare turns
And your lofty beauty is brought low,
When your suffering becomes unending
And pain no remittance shows; →

तवील[1] रातों में तू भी क़रार को[2] तरसे
तेरी निगाह किसी ग़म-गुसार को[3] तरसे
ख़िज़ां-रसीदा-तमन्ना[4] बहार को तरसे
कोई जबीं[5] न तेरे संगे-आस्तां पे[6] झुके !

कि जिन्से-अज्ज़ो-अक़ीदत से[7] तुझको शाद[8] करे
फ़रेबे-वादा-ए-फ़र्दा पे[9] एतिमाद[10] करे
.ख़ुदा वो वक़्त न लाए कि तुझको याद आए—
वो दिल कि तेरे लिए बेक़रार अब भी है
वो आंख जिसको तेरा इन्तिज़ार अब भी है !

Taveel raaton mein tu bhi qaraar ko tarse
teri nigaah kisi ghum-gusaar ko tarse
khizan-rasida-tamanna bahaar ko tarse
Koi jabin na tere sange-aastaan pe jhuke!

Ki jinse-ajzo-aqidat se tujhko shaad kare
farebe-wada-e-pharda pe aitimad kare
Khuda woh waqt na laaye ki tujhko yaad aaye–
Woh dil ki tere liye beqaraar ab bhi hai
woh aankh jisko tera intizaar ab bhi hai !

---

1. लम्बी 2. चैन को 3. सहानुभूति करने वाले को 4. मुर्झाई (विफल) कामना 5. माथा 6. दहलीज़ के पत्थर पर 7. विनय और श्रद्धा से 8. प्रसन्न 9. कल के वायदे के फ़रेब पर 10. विश्वास

May you be spared the long, long nights
When you pine for calm and a comforter need
And your autumnal life yearns for a spring of hope;
May God, the day never comes
When nobody bows at your doorstep,

Nobody pays obeisance and makes you glad
And you are desperately looking for someone
Who can believe your promises false;
May God, you never miss
The heart that beats for you even now,
The eye that is still looking forward to meeting you!

हम कि ठहरे अजनबी इतनी मुलाकातों के बाद
फिर बनेंगे आशना[1] कितनी मुलाकातों के बाद

कब नज़र में आएगी बेदाग़ सब्ज़ा[2] की बहार
खून के धब्बे धुलेंगे कितनी बरसातों के बाद

थे बहुत बेदर्द लम्हे खत्मे-दर्दे-इश्क के
थीं बहुत बेमहर सुबहें मेहरबां रातों के बाद

दिल तो चाहा पर शिकस्ते-दिल[3] ने मोहलत ही न दी
कुछ गिले-शिकवे भी कर लेते मनाजातों[4] के बाद

Hum ki thehre ajnabi itnee mulakaton ke baad
phir banenge aashna kitnee mulakaton ke baad

Kab nazar mein aayegi bedaag sabza ki bahaar
khoon ke dhabbe dhulenge kitnee barsaton ke baad

The bahut bedard lamhe khatme-darde-ishq ke
thin bahut bemehar subhen meharban raaton ke baad

Dil to chaha per shikaste-dil ne mohlat hi na di
kuchh giley-shikve bhi kar letey manajaaton ke baad

---

1. परिचित 2. हरियाली 3. दिल का बुरा हाल 4. मान-मुनव्वल

After so many meetings, we, who stranger remain
After how many more meetings, shall we be familiar again

When will spotless greenery greet the eye again
How many rains will it take to wash the blood-stains

The end of love-affair was truly a painful end
And the days that followed the kindly nights were very hard

I, very much wanted though, the disspririted heart permitted not
To make a complaint or two after beseeching you such a lot

आखिरी ख़त

वो वक़्त मेरी जान बहुत दूर नहीं है
जब दर्द से रुक जायेंगी सब ज़ीस्त[1] की राहें
और हद से गुज़र जायेगा अन्दोहे-निहानी[2]
थक जायेंगी तरसी हुई नाकाम निगाहें
छिन जायेंगे मुझसे मेरे आंसू मेरी आहें
छिन जायेगी मुझसे मेरी बेकार जवानी
शायद मेरी उल्फ़त को बहुत याद करोगी
अपने दिले-मासूम को नाशाद[3] करोगी
आओगी मेरी गोर पे[4] तुम अश्क[5] बहाने
नौख़ेज़[6] बहारों के हसीं फूल चढ़ाने
शायद मेरी तुरबत को[7] भी ठुकरा के चलोगी
शायद मेरी बेसूद वफ़ाओं पे हंसोगी

→

Woh waqt meri jaan bahut door nahin hai
jab dard se ruk jayengi sab zeest ki raahen
aur had se guzar jayega andohe-nihani
thak jayengi tarsi hui nakaam nigahen
chhin jayenge mujhse mere aansu meri aahen
chhin jayegi mujhse meri bekaraar jawani
shayad meri ulphat ko bahut yaad karogi
apne dile-masoom ko nashaad karogi
aaogi meri gor pe tum ashq bahane
naukhej baharon ke hasin phool chadhane
shayad meri turbat ko bhi thukra ke chalogi
shayad meri besood wafhaon pe hansogi

---

1. जीवन 2. भीतरी दुःख 3. दुखित 4. क़ब्र पर 5. आंसू 6. नई 7. क़ब्र को

The Last Letter 

The time is not far, my dear
When the pain inside me will overwhelm me
And choke all paths of life,
When my eyes will be tired of waiting for you,
My youth will have been lost
And I will no longer be able to weep or sigh for your sake
You will perhaps miss my love a lot then
And trouble your innocent heart,
You may then visit my grave,
Pay floral tribute or shed a tear
Or, perhaps trample over it
And mock my miserable love; →

इस वज़'ए-करम का[1] भी तुम्हें पास[2] न होगा
लेकिन दिले-नाकाम को एहसास न होगा

अलक़िस्सा[3] माआले-ग़मे-उल्फ़त पे[4] हंसो तुम
या अश्क़ बहाती रहो, फ़रियाद करो तुम

माज़ी पे[5] नदामत हो तुम्हें या कि मसर्रत
ख़ामोश पड़ा सोएगा बामांदा-ए-उल्फ़त[6]

Is waz-e-karam ka bhi tumhen paas na hoga
lekin diley-nakaam ko ahsaas ne hoga

Alkissa maaley-ghume-ulfat pe hanso tum
ya ashq bahati raho, fariyad karon tum

Maazi pe nadamat ho tumhen ya ki masarrat
khamosh para soega bamanda-e-ulphat

1. कृपा के ढंग का 2. लिहाज़ 3. संक्षेप में यह कि 4. प्रेम के दुःख के परिणाम पर 5. अतीत पर 6. प्रेम के हाथों श्रान्त

You will alas not be aware of what you are doing
And this jilted heart will be sans all feeling;

In short, whether you mock my failed love
Or shed tears and regret your past deeds

Or gloat over them,
Your jilted lover will sleep
Unmindful of it all.

लौहो-कलम

हम परवरिशे-लौहो-कलम[1] करते रहेंगे
जो दिल पे गुज़रती है, रक़म करते रहेंगे[2]
असबाबे-ग़मे-इश्क़[3] वहम[4] करते रहेंगे
वीरानी-ए-दौरां पे[5] करम[6] करते रहेंगे
हां, तल्ख़ी-ए-अय्याम[7] अभी और बढ़ेगी
हां, अहले-सितम[8] मश्क़े-सितम[9] करते रहेंगे
मन्ज़ूर ये तल्ख़ी[10], ये सितम हमको गवारा
दम है तो मदावा-ए-अलम[11] करते रहेंगे
बाक़ी है लहू दिल में तो हर अश्क़ से[12] पैदा
रंगे-लबो-रुख़्सारे-सनम[13] करते रहेंगे
इक तर्ज़े-तग़ाफुल[14] है सो वो उनको मुबारक
इक अर्ज़े तमन्ना[15] है सो हम करते रहेंगे

(जेल में लिखी नज़्म)

Hum parvarishe-loho-kalam karte rahenge
jo dil pe guzarti hai, raqam karte rahenge
asbaabe-ghame-ishq veham karte rahenge
veerani-e-doran pe karam karte rahenge
haan, talkhi-e-ayyam abhi aur badhegi
haan, ahley-sitam mashke-sitam karte rahenge
manzoor ye talkhi, ye sitam humko gawara
dum hai to madava-e-alam karte rahenge
baaki hai lahu dil mein to har ashq se paida
range-labo-rukhsare-sanam karte rahenge
ik tarze-taghaful hai so woh unko mubarak
ik arze tamanna hai so hum karte rahenge

---

1. तख़्ती और क़लम का उपयोग (काव्य-रचना) 2. लिखते रहेंगे 3. इश्क़ के ग़म के साधन 4. जुटाना 5. संसार की वीरानी पर 6. कृपा 7. दिनों (जीवन) की कटुता 8. अत्याचारी 9. अत्याचार करने का अभ्यास 10. कटुता 11. वेदना का इलाज 12. आंसू से 13. प्रेयसी के होंठों और कपोलों का रंग 14. उपेक्षा का ढंग 15. कामना या प्रणय का प्रकटन

Tablet and the Pen 

I shall never cease to record what passes my heart,
And thus keep my pen forever busy...
Never cease to explore the cause of sorrows in love
And thus continue to do a favour to these desolate times.
I know the times are going to be harder still
And the tyrants will do what they do,
I will patiently bear their wrongs and complain not
For, I'm sure, I will have found a cure for every malady in my lifetime itself.

तुम्हारे हुस्न के नाम

सलाम लिखता है शायर तुम्हारे हुस्न के नाम!
बिखर गया जो कभी रंगे-पैरहन[1] सरे-बाम[2]
निखर गई है कभी सुबह, दोपहर, कभी शाम
कहीं जो क़ामते-ज़ेबा पे[3] सज गई है क़बा[4]
चमन में सर्वो-सनोबर[5] संवर गये हैं तमाम
बनी बिसाते-ग़ज़ल[6] जब डुबो लिए दिल ने
तुम्हारे साया-ए-रुख़्सारी-लब में[7] साग़रो-जाम
सलाम लिखता है शायर तुम्हारे हुस्न के नाम!
तुम्हारे हात पे[8] है ताबिशे-हिना[9] जब तक
जहां में बाक़ी है दिलदारिये-उरूसे-सुखन[10]
तुम्हारा हुस्न जवां है तो मेहरबां है फ़लक[11]
तुम्हारा दम है तो दमसाज़[12] है हवा-ए-वतन[13]
अगरचे तंग हैं औक़ात[14] सख़्त हैं आलाम[15]
तुम्हारी याद से शीरीं[16] है तल्ख़ी-ए-अय्याम[17]
सलाम लिखता है शायर तुम्हारे हुस्न के नाम! (जेल में लिखी नज़्म)

Salaam likhta hai shayar tumhare husn ke naam!
Bikhar gaya jo kabhi range-peharan sare-baam
nikhar gai hai kabhi subah, dopehar, kabhi shaam
kahin jo qamte-zeba pe saj gai hai qabaa
chaman mein sarvo-sanobar sanwar gaye hain tamaam
bani bisate-ghazal jab dubo liye dil ne
tumhare saaya-e-rukhsari-lab mein saagaro-jaam
Salaam likhta hai shayar tumhare husn ke naam!
Tumhare haat pe hai tabishe-hina jab tak
jahan mein baaki hai dildariye-uruse-sukhan
tumhara husn jawan hai to meharban hai phalak
tumhara dum hai to damsaaz hai hawa-e-vatan
agarche tang hain auqaat sakht hain aalam
tumhari yaad se shireen hai talkhi-e-ayyaam
Salaam likhta hai shayar tumhare husn ke naam!

To Your Beauty 

The poet salutes your beauty
Whenever the terrace glows with the hues of your dress
Whenever the evening, morning or afternoon look lovely
Whenever your handsome body is decked in beautiful attire
Or the garden is decorated with tall green trees,
When a ghazal is sprouting forth and the heart is intoxicated
With the loveliness of your lips and cheeks—
The poet salutes your beauty.

As long as your palm with mehndi glows
And the charm of poetry works in this world,
As long as the prime of your beauty lasts,
The heavens will be kind;
With you around the climate of my homeland is bracing indeed;
Although the times are hard and suffering acute
The bitterness of life is sweetened by your memory
And the poet salutes your beauty.

---

1. लिबास का रंग 2. छत पर 3. हृदयाकर्षक क़द (शरीर) पर 4. कुर्ता (लिबास) 5. वृक्षों के नाम 6. ग़ज़ल बन गई 7. कपोलों और होंठों की छाया में 8. हाथ पर 9. मेहंदी की आभा 10. कविता-रूपी दुल्हन की दिलदारी 11. आकाश 12. मित्र 13. देश की हवा 14. समय 15. दुःख 16. मधुर 17. जीवन की कटुता

शाहराह

एक अफ़सुर्दा[1] शाहराह[2] है दराज़[3]
दूर उफ़ुक़ पर[4] नज़र जमाए हुए
सर्द मट्टी पे अपने सीने के
सुरमगीं[5] हुस्न को बिछाए हुए

जिस तरह कोई ग़म-ज़दा[6] औरत
अपने वीरां-कदे में[7] महवे-ख़याल[8]
वस्ले-महबूब के[9] तसव्वुर में[10]
मू-ब-मू[11] चूर, उज़्व-उज़्व[12] निढाल

Ek afsurda shaahraah hai daraaz
door uphuq par nazar jamaye hue
sard matti pe apne seene ke
surmagin husn ko bichhaye hue

Jis tarah koi ghum-zada aurat
apne veeran-qade mein mehve-khayal
vasle-mehboob ke tasavur mein
mu-b-mu choor, uzav-uzav nidhal

---

1. उदास 2. राजमार्ग 3. फैला हुआ 4. क्षितिज पर 5. सुरमे के रंग जैसा, कजरारा 6. शोकातुर 7. वीरान घर में 8. विचार-मग्न 9. पिया मिलन के 10. कल्पना में 11. बाल-बाल 12. अंग-अंग

The Highway

A desolate highway
With its gaze fixed on the horizon
And its beauty wrapped in cold earth,
Endlessly stretching—

Like a sad woman,
In her desolate home,
Lost in thoughts of union with her lover,
With each limb, each pore
Aching all over.

राज़े-उल्फ़त छुपाके देख लिया
दिल बहुत कुछ जलाके देख लिया

और क्या देखने को बाक़ी है
आप से दिल लगा के देख लिया

आस उस दर से[1] टूटती ही नहीं
जाके देखा, न जाके देख लिया

वो मेरे होके भी मेरे न हुए
उनको अपना बनाके देख लिया

आज उनकी नज़र में कुछ हमने
सब की नज़रें बचाके देख लिया

Raaze-ulfat chhupake dekh liya
dil bahut kuchh jalake dekh liya

Aur kya dekhne ko baaki hai
aap se dil laga ke dekh liya

Aas us dar se tootti hi nahin
jaake dekha, na jaake dekh liya

Woh mere hoke bhi mere na hue
unko apna banake dekh liya

Aaj unki nazar mein kuchh humne
sab ki nazaren bachake dekh liya

1. दरवाज़े से

My love, I have tried my very best to conceal
And I know how much heartburn doth it feel

I have known what being in love with you doth mean
Is there anything now that remains to be seen ?

I have tried going there, and tried not going.
But hope from that doorstep is no end showing

I made her mine, only to discover
That even when she was mine, she was a stranger

Keeping everybody's eyes at bay
I have seen something in her eyes today

न दीद है न सुखन है न हर्फ़ है न पयाम
कोई भी हीला-ए-तसकीं[1] नहीं और आस बहुत है
उमीद-यार, नज़र का मिज़ाज, दर्द का रंग
तुम आज कुछ भी न पूछो कि दिल उदास बहुत है

Na deed hai na sukhan hai na hurf hai na payaam
koi bhi hila-e-taskin nahin aur aas bahut hai

Umid-yaar, nazar ka mizaaj, dard ka rang
tum aaj kuchh bhi na puchho ki dil udaas bahut hai

1. सांत्वना का ज़रिया

Neither do I see her, nor hear, nor is there a message from her
There is nothing to console me, and yet I expect a lot
About the hope of meeting the friend, the desire of the eye and quality of pain
O ask not, for today I am very sad at heart

इन्तज़ार

गुज़र रहे हैं शबो-रोज़[1] तुम नहीं आतीं
रियाज़े-ज़ीस्त[2] है आज़ुर्दए-बहार[3] अभी
मेरे ख़याल की दुनिया है सोगवार[4] अभी
जो हसरतें[5] तेरे ग़म की कफ़ील[6] हैं प्यारी
अभी तलक मेरी तन्हाइयों में बसती हैं
तवील[7] रातें अभी तक तवील हैं प्यारी
उदास आंखें अभी इन्तिज़ार करती हैं
बहारे-हुस्न[8] पे पाबन्दी-ए-जफ़ा[9] कब तक
ये आज़माइशे-सब्रे-गुरेज़-पा[10] कब तक
क़सम तुम्हारी बहुत ग़म उठा चुका हूं मैं
ग़लत था दावा-ए-सब्रो-शिकेव[11], आ जाओ
क़रारे-ख़ातिरे-बेताब थक गया हूं मैं

Guzar rahe hain shabo-roz tum nahin aatin
Riyaze-zist hai aazurdae-bahaar abhi
mere khayal ki duniya hai sogwar abhi
Jo hasraten tere ghum ki kaphil hain pyari
abhi talak meri tanhaiyon mein basti hain
Taveel raatein abhi tak taveel hain pyari
udaas aankhen abhi intizaar karti hain
Bahaare-husan pe pabandi-e-jafa kab tak
Ye aazmaishe-sabre-gurez-pa kab tak
Qasam tumhari bahut ghum utha chuka hun main
galat tha daawa-e-sabro-shikeve, aa jaao
qarare-khatire-betaab thak gaya hun main

---

1. रात-दिन 2. जीवन का उद्यान 3. वसंत-ऋतु से वंचित 4. शोकपूर्ण 5. अतृप्त आकांक्षाएं 6. ज़मानत 7. लम्बी 8. सौन्दर्य की वसन्त-ऋतु 9. उपेक्षा का बन्धन 10. संघर्ष से बचने की इच्छा रखने वाले धैर्य की परीक्षा 11. धैर्य और सहन-शक्ति की दावा

Waiting

Days and nights roll by, but you have not come
The garden of life is unvisited by spring as yet
And the world of my thought is still sad;
The joys that I got by sorrowing for you
Still in my solitude glow,
The long nights are still very long, my dear
And my wistful eyes wait for you still.
How long will the bloom of beauty with infidelity be associated !
How much longer will my patience be tested?
I have suffered a lot already, I swear by you.
My boast of endurance and patience
Was nothing but a boast,
I am yearning for some peace
Pray, do come now.

हुस्न और मौत

जो फूल सारे गुलिस्तां में सबसे अच्छा हो
फ़ुरोग़े-नूर[1] हो जिससे फ़िज़ाए-रंगी[2] में
ख़िज़ां[3] के जौरो-सितम[4] को न जिसने देखा हो
बहार ने जिसे ख़ूने-जिगर से पाला हो
वो एक फूल समाता है चश्मे-गुलचीं[5] में
हज़ार फूलों से आबाद बाग़े-हस्ती[6] है
अजल[7] की आंख फ़क़त एक को तरसती है
कई दिलों की उम्मीदों का जो सहारा हो
फ़िज़ा-ए-दहर की आलूदगी[8] से बाला[9] हो
जहां में आके अभी जिसने कुछ न देखा हो
नक़्हते-ऐशो-मसर्रत[10], न ग़म की अरज़ानी[11]
किनारे-रहमते-हक़[12] में उसे सुलाती है
सुकूते-शब[13] में फ़रिश्तों की मर्सिया-ख़्वानी[14]
तवाफ़[15] करने को सुबहे-बहार आती है
सबा[16] चढ़ाने को जन्नत के फूल लाती है

Jo phool saare gulistan mein sabse achha ho
phuroge-noor ho jisse phizaye-rangi mein
Khizan ke zoro-sitam ko na jisne dekha ho
bahaar ne jise khoone-jigar se pala ho
woh ek phool samata hai chashme-gulchi mein
Hazaar phoolon se abaad bage-hasti hai
ajal ki aankh phaqat ek ko tarasti hai
kai dilon ki ummidon ka jo sahara ho
fiza-e-dehar ki aaludgi se baala ho
Jahan mein aake abhi jisne kuchh na dekha ho
nakehte-aisho-masarrat na ghum ki arzaani
kinare-rehmate-huq mein use sulati hai
sukute-shab mein farishton ki marsiya-khawani
tavaf karne ko subhe-bahaar aati hai
saba chadhane ko jannat ke phool laati hai

Beauty and Death 

The finest flower in the garden that makes the
colourful atmosphere more colourful still
Nursed by the spring with its own life blood
And unknown to the cruelty of autumn yet—
That is the flower that the gardener aims at.
In the garden of life, a thousand flowers bloom
But death longs for only one of them—
The one that sustains hope in every heart,
The one that has not been corrupted by the world
around,
Which as yet has seen very little of the world
Which neither for want of comfort nor for excess
of sorrow though,
Sleeps in God's benign lap,
The one for whom the angels pray in the silence of
night
The one for whom the spring itself come for a
pilgrimage
And the morning breeze brings fresh buds from
heaven to worship.

---

1. प्रकाश में बढ़ोतरी 2. रंगीन वातावरण 3. पतझड़ 4. अत्याचार और क्रूरता 5. फूल चुननेवाले की दृष्टि 6. जीवन रूपी उद्यान 7. मृत्यु 8. सृष्टि के वातावरण की लिप्ति 9. उच्च (निर्लिप्त) 10. ऐश्वर्य एवं सुख की कमी 11. दुःखों की बहुलता 12. ईश्वर की कृपा रूपी गोद 13. रात की निस्तब्धता 14. शोक-गीत 15. परिक्रमा 16. प्रभात-समीर

ये लहू की महक है कि लबे-यार की खुशबू
किस राह की जानिब से सबा आई है देखो
गुलशन में बहार आई कि ज़िंदां[1] हुआ आबाद
किस सिम्त[2] से नग़मों की सदा आई है देखो

Ye lahoo ki mehak hai ki labe-yaar ki khushboo
kis raah ki janib se saba aai hai dekho
Gulshan mein bahaar aai ki zindan hua abaad
kis simt se naghmon ki sada aai hai dekho

1. जेलखाना, 2. दिशा

Is it the smell of blood or fragrance from the friend's lips
From which side has the breeze come, please, see
Has the spring come in the garden or new inmates come to the prison
From which side the notes of a song come, find out, prithee.

पास रहो

तुम मेरे पास रहो
मेरे क़ातिल, मेरे दिलदार, मेरे पास रहो,
जिस घड़ी रात चले,
आसमानों का लहू पी के सियाह रात चले
मरहमे-मुश्क लिए,[1] नश्तरे-अलमास [2] लिये
वैन करती हुई, हंसती हुई, गाती हुई निकले
दर्द के कासनी पाज़ब बजाती निकले,
जिस घड़ी सीने में डूबे हुए दिल
आस्तीनों में निहां[3] हाथों की राह तकने लगे,
आस लिये
और बच्चों के तड़पने की तरह कलकले-मय [4]
बहरे-नासूदगी मचले तो मनाये न मने
जब कोई बात बनाये न बने,
जिस घड़ी मातमी, सुनसान सियाह रात चले
पास रहो
मेरे क़ातिल, मेरे दिलदार, मेरे पास रहो।

Tum mere paas raho
mere qaatil, mere dildar, mere paas raho
jis ghari raat chale
aasmano ka lahoo peekey siyah raat chale
marhum-e-mushk liye nashtare-almaas liya
vain karti hui, hansti hui, gaati hui nikle
dard ke kaasni paazeb bajati nikle
jis ghari seene mein doobe hue dil
aasteenon mein nihan haathon ki rah takne lage
aas liye
aur bachchon ke tarapne ki tarah kalkale-mai
behre-nasoodgi machle to manaye na mane
jab koi baat banaye na bane
jis ghari maatmi, susaan siyah raat chale
paas raho
mere qaatil, mere dildar, mere paas raho

---

1. कस्तूरी की खुशबू 2. नश्तर लगाने का नुकीला चाकू 3. छिपा हुआ 4. शराब से गरारा करने की आवाज़

Be Near Me

Be near me,
My assassin, my love, be by my side
When this dark night, drinking the blood of the skies
advances,
When this night advances
Carrying with it the fragrant balm of the diamond
lancet,
At once, wailing, singing and laughing,
Tinkling the purple anklet of pain,
When hearts, sinking in the bosom.
Look wistfully for hands, hidden in the sleeves,
When the wine-gargle-like whining of the children
Once started, stops not
When no device works,
Be near me
When the desolate, dark and mourning night
advances.
My assassin, my love, be by my side.

कोई आशिक़ किसी महबूब से

गुलशन-ए याद में गर आज दम-ए-बाद-ए-सबा[1]
फिर से चाहे कि गुल-अफशाँ[2] हो तो हो जाने दो
उम्र-ए-रफ्ता[3] के किसी ताक पे बिसरा हुआ दर्द
फिर से चाहे कि फ़रोज़ाँ[4] हो तो हो जाने दो
जैसे बेगाने से अब मिलते हो वैसे ही सही
आओ दो-चार घड़ी मेरे मुक़ाबिल बैठो
गरचि मिल बैठेंगे हम तुम तो मुलाक़ात के बाद
अपना एहसास-ए-ज़याँ[5] और ज़ियादा होगा
हम-सुख़न[6] होंगे जो हम दोनों तो हर बात के बीच
अनकही बात का मौहूम[7] सा परदा होगा
कोई इक़रार न मैं याद दिलाऊँगा न तुम
कोई मज़मून वफ़ा का न जफा का होगा
गर्दे अय्याम की तहरीर को धोने के लिए
तुम से गोया हों दमे-दीद जो मेरी पलकें
तुम जो चाहो तो सुनो और जो न चाहो न सुनो
और जो हर्फ करें मुझसे गुरेज़ा आँखें
तुम जो चाहो तो कहो और जो न चाहो न कहो

Gulshan-e-yaad mein gar aaj dum-e-baad-e-saba
phir se chahe ki gul-afshan ho to ho jaane do
umre-e-rafta ke kisi taak pe bisra hua dard
phir se chahe ki pharozan ho to ho jaane do
jaise begane se ab milte ho vaise hi sahi
aao do-char ghari mere muqabil baitho
garchi mil baithenge hum tum to mulakat ke baad
apna ahsaas-e-zayaan aur ziyada hoga
hum-sukhan honge jo hum dono to har baat ke beech
ankahi baat ka mauhoom sa parda hoga
koi iqraar na main yaad dilaunga na tum
koi mazmoon wafa ka na jafa ka hoga
garde ayyam ki tehreer ko dhone ke liye
tum se goya hon dume-deed jo meri palken
tum jo chaho to suno aur jo na chaho na suno
aur jo hurf karen mujhse gureza aankhen
tum jo chaho to kaho aur jo na chaho na kaho

A Lover to his Beloved

If the morning breeze once again wants to shower
flowers
In the memory's garden, let it do so,
If some pain, put away in some niche of the past
Longs to be kindled again, be it so;
Like a stranger meets a stranger
Come and sit before me for a while.
There will be no mention of any commitment and
callousness
Nor will I remind you of any promises, made in the
past,
Although when we sit together again
Our sense of loss after the meeting will be greater
And something will always remain unsaid, when we
speak.
And if in order to wash away the dust of the past
My eyes say something when I glance at you
It is upto you to listen or not to listen,
And if your evasive eyes want to censure me in
some way
You are quite free to say whatever you want to say.

1. पवन का झोंका 2. फूल बिखराना 3. बीती हुई उम्र 4. उज्ज्वल, रोशन 5. खोने की अनुभूति 6. दूसरे से बात करते हुए 7. आशंकित, हलका-सा

फिलिस्तीनी बच्चों के नाम

मत रो बच्चे
रो-रो के अभी
तेरी अम्मी की आँख लगी है
मत रो बच्चे
कुछ ही पहले
तेरे अब्बा ने
अपने ग़म से रुखसत[1] ली है
मत रो बच्चे
तेरा भाई
अपने ख्वाब की तितली पीछे
दूर कहीं परदेस गया है
मत रो बच्चे
तेरी बाजी[2] का
डोला पराये देस गया है
मत रो बच्चे, →

Mat ro bachche
ro-ro ke abhi
teri ammi ki aankh lagi hai
Mat ro bachche
kuchh hi pehle
tere abba ne
apne ghum se rukhsat lee hai
Mat ro bachche
tera bhai
apne khwab ki titlee pichhe
door kahin pardes gaya hai
Mat ro bachche
teri baaji ka dola paraye des gaya hai
Mat ro bachche,

---

1. अवकाश 2. बहन

Lullaby to the Palestinian Children 

Do not cry, my child
Your mother has just slept after weeping a long while,

Do not cry, my child
Only some time back, your father has departed
Relieved of all sorrow,
Do not cry my child,
Your brother is away to an alien land
And your sister has gone away the same way,
Do not cry my child, →

तेरे आँगन में
मुर्दा सूरज नहला के गये हैं
चन्द्रमा दफ़ना के गये हैं
मत रो बच्चे
अम्मी, अब्बा, बाजी, भाई
चाँद और सूरज
तू गर रोयेगा तो ये सब
और भी तुझको रुलवायेंगे
तू मुस्कायेगा तो शायद
सारे एक दिन भेस बदलकर
तुझसे खेलने लौट आयेंगे।

Tere aangan mein
murda suraj nehla ke gaye hain
chandrama dafna ke gaye hain
Mat ro bachche
ammi, abba, baaji, bhai
chand aur suraj
to gar royega to ye sab
aur bhi tujhko rulvayenge
tu muskayega to shayad
saare ek din bhes badalkar
tujhse khelne laut aayenge

They have just bathed the dead sun and buried the
moon in your courtyard,

Do not cry my child,
For, if you cry,
Your mother, father, brother and sister
Alongwith the sun and the moon
Will make you cry all the more.

And if you smile
There is a real possibility
That all of them in disguise
Will come and play with you.

ऐ रोशनियों के शहर

सब्ज़ा[1]-सब्ज़ा सूख रही है फीकी ज़रद[2] दुपहर
दीवारों को चाट रहा है तन्हाई का ज़हर
दूर उफ़क़[3] तक घटती-बढ़ती, उठती-गिरती रहती है
कहर की सूरत बेरौनक दर्दों की गंदली लहर
बसता है इस कहर के नीचे रोशनियों का शहर
ऐ रोशनियों के शहर
कौन कहे किस सिम्त[4] है तेरी रोशनियों की राह
हर जानिब बेनूर खड़ा है हिज्र का शहर पनाह
थककर हर सू बैठ रही है शौक की मांद सियाह[5]
आज मेरा दिल फिक्र में है
ऐ रोशनियों के शहर
शब खूं से मुँह फेर न जाये अरमानों की रौ
खैर हो तेरी लैलाओं की, उन सब से कह दो
आज की शब जब दिये जलाये, ऊँची रक्खैं लौ।

Sabza-sabza sookh rahi hai phiki zarad dopehar
diwaaron ko chaat raha hai tanhai ka zahar
door uphaq tak ghati-badhti, uthti-girti rehti hai
qahar ki surat beraunak dardon ki gandali lehar
basta hai is qahar ke niche roshniyon ka shehar
ai roshniyon ke shehar
kaun kahe kis simt hai teri roshniyon ki raah
har janib benoor khara hai hizra ka shehar panaah
Thak kar har su baith rahi hai shauq ki maand siyaah
aaj mera dil phikra mein hai
ai roshniyon ke shehar
shab khoon se munha pher na jaaye armaano ki rau
khair ho teri lailaon ki, un sab se keh do
aaj ki shab jab diye jalayen, unchi rakhen lau

---

1. हरियाली 2. पीली 3. क्षितिज 4. दिशा 5. थकी हुई फौज

O City of Lights

All greenery is withering away in the dull and pale noon
The walls are being eaten up by the termite of loneliness
A listless, dull pain rises and falls doomlike
All the way to the distant horizon...
And beyond this veil lies the city of lights.

O city of lights,
Who can tell me how to reach you,
Which is the way!
For, on every side, stand
Dark forbidding walls
And the forces of hope
Are sitting dismayed.

My heart is heavy today
O city of lights,
Lest the onslaught of night should drive away
The forces of hope,
— I wish them well—
Tell your Lailas, pray
To keep the lights of their candle bright
Tonight.

मेरे दिल, मेरे मुसाफ़िर

मेरे दिल, मेरे मुसाफ़िर
हुआ फिर से हुक्म सादिर[1]
कि वतन-बदर[2] हों हम तुम
दें गली-गली सदाएँ
करें रुख नगर-नगर का
कि सुराग़ कोई पाएँ
किसी यार-ए-नामा-बर[3] का
हर एक अजनबी से पूछें
जो पता था अपने घर का
सर-ए-कू-ए-नाशनायाँ[4]
हमें दिन से रात करना

Mere dil, mere musafir
hua phir se huqam saadir
ki vatan-badar hon hum tum
den gali-gali sadayen
karen rukh nagar-nagar ka
ki suraag koi paayen
kisi yaar-e-nama-bar ka
har ek ajnabi se poochen
jo pata tha apne ghar ka
sar-e-ku-e-nashnayaan
humein din se raat karna

---

1. घोषित 2. देश-निकाला 3. पत्रवाहक 4. अजनबी गलियों में

My Journeyman Heart

Again the orders are issued,
O my journeyman heart
That we go into exile;
Move from town to town
Call out from every street
For some friendly messenger
And on alien soil
Far way from home
Ask every stranger
The address of our own house.

दरीचे

गड़ी हैं कई सलीबें मेरे दरीचे में
हर एक अपने मसीहा के खून का रंग लिये
हर एक वसले-खुदावंद[1] की उमंग लिये

किसी पे करते हैं अब्रे-बहार[2] को कुरबां
किसी पे कत्ल मये-ताबनाक[3] करते हैं
किसी पे होती है सरमस्त शाखसार दो नीम
किसी पे बादे-सबा को लाहलाक[4] करते हैं

हर आये दिन ये खुदावंदगाने महरो-जमाल
लहू में गर्म मेरे ग़म-कदे[5] में आते हैं
और आये दिन मेरी नज़रों के सामने इनके
शहीद जिस्म सलामत उठाये जाते हैं।

Gari hain kai salibein mere dariche mein
har ek apne masiha ke khoon ka rang liye
har ek vasle-khudavand ki umang liye

Kisi pe karte hain abre-bahaar ko kurban
kisi pe qatl maye-taabnaak karte hain
kisi pe hoti hai sarmast shakhsaar do neem
kisi badey-saba ko laahlaak karte hain

Har aaye din ye khudavandgaane mehro-jamaal
lahoo mein garm mere gham-kade mein aate hain
aur aaye din meri nazron ke saamne inke
shaheed zism salamat uthaye jaate hain

---

1. ईश्वर से मिलाप 2. बहार का बादल 3. शोख शराब 4. कत्ल 5. ग़मग़ीन घर

Windows 

Many a cross is fixed on my window
Each one of them soaked in blood of the messiah,
Each one of them longing to meet its god;

On the one is mutilated the spring-cloud
On the other is slain the shining moon,
If on the third, the fruit-laden boughs are beheaded
The morning breeze is murdered on the forth.

Everyday gods of grace and beauty
Come to my sorrowland soaked in blood
And right before my eyes each day
Their mortified bodies are taken away.

जब तेरी समुन्दर आंखों में

ये धूप-किनारा शाम ढले
मिलते हैं दोनों वक्त जहाँ
जो रात न दिन, जो आज न कल
पल भर को अमर, पल भर में धुआँ
होटों की लपक
बाहों की छनक
ये मेल हमारा, झूठ न सच
क्यों राड़[1] करो, क्यों दोष धरो
किस कारण झूठी बात करो
जब तेरी समन्दर आँखों में
इस शाम का सूरज डूबेगा
सुख सोयेंगे घर-दर वाले
और राही अपनी राह लेगा।

Ye dhoop-kinara shaam dhale
milte hain dono waqt jahan
jo raat na din, jo aaj na kal
pal bhar ko amar, pal bhar mein dhuan
honton ki lapak
bahon ki chhanak
ye male humara, jhooth na such
kyon raar karo, kyon dosh dharo
kis karan jhoothi baat karo
jab teri samandar aankhon mein
is shaam ka suraj doobega
sukh soyenge ghar-dar wale
aur raahi apni raah lega

1. झगड़ा

In Your Ocean-like Eyes 

A momentary smoky interval.
When the two hours of time meet,
When it is neither day nor night
Neither tomorrow nor today,
On this fringe of the day
This quivering of the lips, this tinkling in the arm
This momentary union, neither true nor false—
At such a time, why do you crib, what for quarrel?
Soon, the evening sun will set in your ocean-like eyes,
The householders peacefully sleep
And this traveller wend his way.

रात यूं दिल में तेरी खोई हुई याद आई
जैसे वीराने में चुपके-से बहार आ जाये
जैसे सहराओं[1] में चलने लगे बादे-नसीम
जैसे बीमार को बेवज़ह क़रार आ जाये

Raat yun dil mein teri khoi hui yaad aai
jaise veerane mein chupke-se bahaar aa jaaye
Jaise sahraon mein chalne lage baade-naseem
jaise bimaar ko bevazah qaraar aa jaaye

1. रेगिस्तानों

Like the arrival of spring suddenly in desolate county,
Like the morning breeze blowing quietly through the
desert land
Like a patient unexpectedly feeling alright
Your memory crossed my mind last night.

तेरा जमाल[1] निगाहों में लेके उट्ठा हूँ
निखर गयी है फ़िज़ा तेरे पैरहन[2] की तरह
नसीम तेरे शबिस्तां[3] से होके आयी है
मेरी सहर में ख़ुशबू है तेरे बदन की तरह

Tera jamaal nigahon mein leke uttha hun
nikhar gayi hai fiza tere perhan ki tarah
naseem tere shabistan se hoke aayi hai
meri sehar mein khushboo hai tere badan ki tarah

---

1. सौन्दर्य 2. पहरावा 3. सोने का कमरा

I rise with my eyes filled with your beauty
The dawn, like your garment, glows
The breeze is coming as if wafted from your
bed chamber
And through the air the fragrance of your body flows

कुत्ते

ये गलियों के आवारा बेकार कुत्ते
कि बख़्शा गया जिनको ज़ौक़े-गदाई[1]
ज़माने की फटकार सरमाया[2] इनका
जहां-भर की दुतकार इनकी कमाई
न आराम शब को न राहत सवेरे
ग़लाज़त में[3] घर, नालियों में बसेरे
जो बिगड़ें तो इक दूसरे से लड़ा दो
ज़रा एक रोटी का टुकड़ा दिखा दो
ये हर एक की ठोकरें खाने वाले
ये फ़ाक़ों से उकता के मर जाने वाले
ये मज़लूम मख़्लूक़[4] गर सर उठाये
तो इन्सान सब सरकशी[5] भूल जाये
ये चाहें तो दुनिया को अपना बना लें
ये आक़ाओं की[6] हड्डियां तक चबा लें
कोई इनको एहसासे-ज़िल्लत[7] दिला दे
कोई इनकी सोई हुई दुम हिला दे

Ye galiyon ke awara bekaar kutte
ki baksha gaya jinko zaukey-gadaai
zamane ki fatkaar sarmaya inka
jahan-bhar ki dutkaar inki kamaai
na aaram shab ko na rahat savere
ghalazat mein ghar, naliyon mein basere
jo bigrein to ik dusare se lara do
zara ek roti ka tukra dikha do
ye her ek ki thokrein khane wale
ye phakon se ukta ke mar jaane wale
ye mazloom makhlook gar sar uthaye
to insaan sab sarkashi bhool jaaye
ye chahen to duniya ko apna bana lein
ye aakaaon ki haddiyon tak chaba lein
koi inko ahsaase-zillat dila de
koi inki soi hui dum hila de

Dogs

These stray dogs, loitering about in the streets
Living on beggary
Being stoned away by everybody
And rebuked by all and sundry—
They have no rest at night, no respite by day;
Tempt them with a loaf of bread
And make them fight each other if they became
inconvenient
Kicked about by everybody
And ultimately starving to death,
This oppressed populace, however, if it ever rises
in revolt
They would show the haughty ones their place,
Eat up their tormentors alive
And make this world all their own—
If only somebody roused them shaking them by
their tail,
If only somebody made them realize the disgrace
in which they live!

---

1. भीख मांगने की रुचि 2. निधि 3. गंदगी में 4. जनता 5. घमण्ड 6. मालिकों की 7. अपमान की अनुभूति

तमाम शब[1] दिल-वहशी[2] तलाश करता है
हर एक सदा[3] में तेरे हर्फ़े-लुत्फ़ का आहंग[4]
हर एक सुबह मिलाती है बार-बार नज़र
तेरे दहन[5] से लाला-ओ-गुलाब का रंग

Tamaam shab dil-vehshi talash karta hai
har ek sada mein tere herphe-lutph ka aahang
har ek subah milati hai baar-baar nazar
tere dehan se lala-o-gulab ka rang

1. रात 2. पागल दिल 3. आवाज़ 4. लय 5. मुँह

All night, the mad heart
Looks for the rhythm of your speech in every sound,
And every morning, my eyes are exerting to see
If in the rose and the tulip, the glow of your face
can be found

दिल में अब यूं तेरे भूले हुए ग़म आते हैं
जैसे बिछड़े हुए का'बे में सनम[1] आते हैं

एक-एक करके हुए जाते हैं तारे रोशन
मेरी मंज़िल की तरफ़ तेरे क़दम आते हैं

कुछ हमीं को नहीं एहसान उठाने का दिमाग़
वो तो जब आते हैं, माइल-ब-करम[2] आते हैं

और कुछ देर न गुज़रे शबे-फुर्क़त[3] से कहो
दिल भी कम दुखता है वो याद भी कम आते हैं

(जेल में लिखी नज़्म)

Dil mein ab yun tere bhoole hue ghum aatey hain
jaise bichhre hue kaabe mein sanam aatey hain

Ek-ek karke hue jaate hain tarey roshan
meri manzil ki taraf tere kadam aatey hain

Kuchh hamin ko nahin ahsaan uthane ka dimaag
woh to jab aatey hain, maail-b-karam aatey hain

Aur kuchh der na guzrey shabe-phurkat se kaho
dil bhi kam dukhta hai woh yaad bhi kam aatey hain

1. मूर्तियां 2. कृपा करने पर उतारू 3. वियोग की रात

As foresaken idols there way back to the Kaaba find
Your forgotten sorrows now cross my mind

The stars are appearing in the sky one by one
As, step by step, you are moving towards me, your
destination

He is willing to oblige as ever
Only, I am not inclined to take anybody's favour

Let the night of separation, a little longer last
For, the heart is aching less and my remembrance
of her is not as frequent as in the past.

अब वही हर्फ़े-जुनूं[1] सब की ज़बां ठहरी है
जो भी चल निकली है, वो बात कहां ठहरी है

आज तक शैख़ के अकराम में[2] जो शै थी हराम
अब वही दुश्मने-दीं[3] राहते-जां[4] ठहरी है

वस्ल की शब थी तो किस दर्जा सुबक[5] गुज़री थी
हिज्र की शब है तो क्या सख्त गिरां[6] ठहरी है

इक दफ़ा बिखरी तो हात आई है कब मौजे-शमीम[7]
दिल से निकली है तो क्या लब पे फ़ुग़ां[8] ठहरी है

आते-आते युंही दम-भर को रुकी होगी बहार
जाते-जाते युंही पल-भर को ख़िज़ां ठहरी है

हमने तो तर्ज़े-फ़ुग़ां[9] की है क़फ़स में[10] ईजाद[11]
'फ़ैज़' गुलशन में वही तर्ज़े-बयां[12] ठहरी है

(जेल में लिखी नज़्म)

Ab wahi hurphe-junoon sab ki zaban thehri hai
jo bhi chal nikli hai, woh baat kahan thehri hai
aaj tak sheikh ke akraam mein jo shai thi haraam
ab wahi dushman-e-din raahte-jaan thehri hai
vasl ki shab thi to kis darja subak guzri thi
hizra ki shab hai to kya sakht giran thehri hai
ik dapha bikhri to haat aai hai kab mauje-shameem
dil se niklee hai to kya lab pe phugan thehri hai
aatey-aatey yunhi dam-bhar ko ruki hogi bahaar
jatey-jatey yunhi pal-bhar ko khizan thehri hai
humne to tarze-phugan ki hai kafas mein ijaad
'Faiz' gulshan mein vahi tarze-bayan thehri hai

---

1. उन्माद की बात (भाषा) 2. पारितोषिक में 3. धर्म की शत्रु 4. जीवन का आनन्द 5. हलकी, 6. भारी, असह्य 7. सुगन्धि की लहर 8. होंठों पर आह 9. आर्त्तनाद का ढंग 10. पिंजरे (जेल) में 11. आविष्कार 12. बात का ढंग

The same language of passion is now spoken
everywhere
What is started once, can seldom be stopped, if ever

That which has so far been a taboo in the eyes of
the preacher
The same sin, in religion, turns out to be a source
of comfort and life-giver

When it was the night of union, time simply sped past
And the night of separation seems a whole century
to last

Once diffused, a wave of fragrance is never
recaptured
A sigh, once it leaves the heart cannot be withheld

The spring must not have stopped for more than a
while when it came.
And when the autumn departed, the story was just
the same

The vehicle to ventilate my sorrow which I invented
while in the prison
Has, in the garden become a mode of expression,
O Faiz with everyone

❏

www.ingramcontent.com/pod-product-compliance
Lightning Source LLC
Chambersburg PA
CBHW031422090925
32260CB00031B/1145/J
* 9 7 8 8 1 7 0 2 8 7 9 1 9 *